Dear Tiffany

I pray that His
would be fulfilled in ways beyond
expectation & hopes

THE PROMISE
OF THE
PRESENCE

Rebuilding the Tabernacle of David

blessings and peace

ALUN LEPPITT

RIVER
PUBLISHING

River Publishing & Media Ltd
Barham Court
Teston
Maidstone
Kent
ME18 5BZ
United Kingdom

info@river-publishing.co.uk

ISBN 978-1-908393-49-4
Cover design by www.spiffingcovers.com
Printed in the United Kingdom

CONTENTS

DEDICATION

This book is dedicated to every passionate
worshipper on the planet.

ACKNOWLEDGEMENTS

To my God – Heavenly Father, King Jesus and Holy Spirit. My heart is transformed from glory to glory by encounters with your magnificent grace and perfect love.

My wife Donna, my true companion and best friend. For your sacrificial prayers and being a rock of strength through the storms, you are an amazing blessing, not just to me but to the nations.

Love, hugs and blessings always to my family, especially my daughter Naomi and my Dad, whose love and generosity continually touch my heart.

I would like to honour a spiritual father, Pastor Gary Kantola (Our Father's House, Pennsylvania, USA). He hosted the Tabernacle of David worship conferences and was a wonderful man of deep integrity, with an inspiring passion for God: a kingdom warrior sorely missed.

I've had the privilege of working with so many wonderful musicians and singers over thirty years. There are too many names to mention, but some of the most significant times of my life have been making a heavenly sound with you.

Dr. Randy Clark – your inspiration, teaching and anointing is truly remarkable. Like thousands of others my life changed forever after the laying on of hands by a faithful father of revival. God bless you as you bless the nations.

Dr. Tom Jones and the Global Awakening family – your pioneering, training, equipping and empowering continues to bring transformation across the world.

To Bethel Redding and Bethel Music – when I came to your house, I came home. The vision of my heart was manifested in all you do – simply beautiful. I've listened to 'Without Words' for hours while writing this manuscript ... thank you for your excellence!

Ade Lovegrove – you are a man of great depth and wisdom. Thank you for our years of journeying together and your valuable input in the development of material for this book.

Finally, to my Bridge family in Southampton – every message, every moment hosting his presence together, every encounter, every time God came near has been wonderfully amazing. It is stunning what we have witnessed together over the years. May the Father's blessing and favour be over us!

FOREWORD

The Promise of the Presence: Rebuilding the Tabernacle of David is an encouraging read. It provides insights into many important issues related to church life, but especially that of worship and praise, and their power to usher in the presence of God for prophecy, healing and miracles.

Many years ago I was awakened suddenly and heard a strong internal voice from God: "When my presence is in your midst, so is my power to heal the sick!" I have found this to be absolutely true. Alun, too, has discovered this truth and writes about it here. His book makes a strong connection between presence and power, and the important role that worship plays in bringing the presence of God into the sanctuary. Worship helps to establish the Lord's presence as Healer, Deliverer and Saviour.

Alun emphasises the great invitation: draw near to God and He will draw near to us. This results in a life-changing experience that prepares us to better fulfil the first and second great commandments and the great commission.

Alun's book helps us to see that the fruit of our faithfulness is greater favour with God. Or as I understand it, obedience and faithfulness result in intimacy, and intimacy results in revelation, and revelation results in faith, and faith results in a greater manifestation of His power.

It is interesting that in the Assembly in Acts 15, the Apostle James refers to the restoration of the Tabernacle of David. This is strategic and important for us to understand. Alun helps us to see the importance of the restoration of the kind of worship that occurred in the Tabernacle of David and how prophetic it was for the New Testament Church. God is restoring this kind of worship in our day.

This is not just a book for your worship team or the choir, however, it is for the entire church. Because as a corporate body of God's people, our worship has the ability to shift the spiritual atmosphere, resulting in the release of captives, the healing of the sick, the release of miraculous provision, and the manifestation of His presence.

Alun helps us to understand that this kind of worship is not a ritual or a formality, but rather true worshippers hunger for more of the Eternal One. They would worship for the Audience of One, even if no one else was in the sanctuary. He reminds us that the Old Testament emphasis of the biblical tabernacles and Solomon's temple being a place for God to call "home" has been superseded by the New Testament emphasis of God becoming present in the midst of a passionate people.

I have seen Alun worshipping God with passion. I have listened to his heart as he talks about worship and its importance. This book is not a theoretical book, but has been written from the hand of a practitioner, not merely a theoretician. I highly recommend it for individual study, for small group study, for use in Sunday School classes and for retreats.

Dr Randy Clark
Overseer of the Apostolic Network of Global Awakening

PREFACE

Over thirty years ago my sole dream as a skinny, long-haired teenager was to become a rock star. Then a life-changing revelation propelled me in an unexpected direction. I glimpsed something in a moment that I would eagerly pursue for the rest of my life. It was all about worship.

God imprinted a vision for corporate worship on my DNA. I saw how we would gather and worship God in such an abandoned and passionate way that he would draw near to us, as promised in James 4:8. There he would pour out his abundant blessings on a people after his own heart.

In this vision his manifest presence was so tangible, so real, and so heavy. As people came into that environment they would meet with the Creator of the universe as their loving heavenly Dad and be touched, transformed, healed and set free...

Such a thing was far from my experience. I had grown up reluctantly attending the local Anglican church, where my Mum led the Sunday school. As a young boy I didn't understand why I had to go to school on a Sunday morning, when I'd been in class all week. It just got in the way of playing football or cricket!

In those services, I didn't know when to stand up and when to sit down. Worship meant numbers on a wooden board and singing long, boring hymns to a droning pipe organ. I certainly didn't understand the thees, thous and vouchsafests. I would agree with Adrian Plass when he describes the traditional hymnal Ancient and Modern as Hymns Ancient and Prehistoric!

My mum used to keep me quiet with a colouring book or a comic and I watched the clock until I could get home. My brother got so distracted one service that he managed to get his finger stuck in a hole in a pew. We had to remove him and the pew from the church before he could be cut free!

Lights on

The light went on for me when I was 15, after much nagging and my mum's persistent prayers. I got to know a group of young people who knew Jesus personally and went to a Christian fellowship where they sang songs in a large circle with a piano and an acoustic guitar. The tunes were simple and catchy and the whole thing was fun and friendly. There was a life in it I couldn't put into words and all the people there seemed happy and real.

At the time I didn't know it was called the charismatic renewal; I was just glad to be part of something authentic and meaningful, and to discover a stirring in my heart I hadn't known was there. I experienced tingling over my body in those meetings which I later discovered was the presence of God. Most importantly, I found Jesus in a way that transformed me from the inside out. It changed the way I was thinking and started me on a very special journey.

I knew from an early age I wanted to be a musician, or at least a drummer! When I fell in love with Jesus, playing music and writing songs became a way of expressing what I believed and was starting to experience. I introduced drums to our little fellowship, and after the initial 'Ohh, it's a bit loud,' people got used to the noisy youth in the corner with the worship band.

My patient parents let me put up my drum set in my bedroom and bash away as my friends and I formed the band to end all bands. We must have made the most awful racket! During one legendary practice session, a neighbour from almost a block away asked us to turn it down. Well, we were playing rock music and there is only one setting on the amplifiers for that!

In drumming, music and song-writing, I suddenly found a part of me that had never before really had a voice. Scripture, the Sunday messages, conferences and life experiences all wove their way into my lyrics and melodies. Many years before I stood up and preached my first sermon, I delivered truth encased in music.

I used to bring my latest offerings to the unsuspecting youth at our monthly event called Interface. I even went into a studio with some of the Delirious boys in those early days and made an album of songs released on that great medium of the past, cassette tapes. Worship and song-writing became a huge focus for me. I discovered who I was and my primary calling ... to be a worshipper.

1

THE BIRTH OF A VISION

My journey as a worshipper began. I had a hunger in my heart to play music, to write music and to worship with an abandon and enthusiasm that used to scare the older people. Beneath my shy exterior stands a roaring lion! I started to study the scriptures and grow in my understanding of worship. I spent a long time in the Psalms and reading about King David. He soon became a hero of the faith for me as I looked at some of those Sunday school stories with fresh eyes.

Then one day, I was spending time in the company of the so-called 'minor prophets' of the Old Testament and got stuck in Amos. Chapter nine seemed to contain hidden treasure in its words about God's intention to rebuild his fallen tabernacle. It was like a lightning strike from heaven in my heart. Long before I fully understood its meaning, this passage had a deep impact on me.

Revelation came as I read, as if the text on the page was highlighted and lifted up before my eyes, glowing like fire. Something about this decree from the shepherd-prophet resonated in my inmost being. I knew it was the voice of God and scribbled notes as I read it again:

'On that day I will raise up the tabernacle of David, which has fallen down, and repair its damages; I will raise up its ruins, and rebuild it as in the days of old; that they may possess the remnant of Edom, and all the Gentiles who are

called by my name,' says the LORD who does this thing. (Amos 9:11–12 NKJV)

God was declaring his intent to do again what he had done with King David. I knew that David was a worshipper and a man after God's heart, but here in this passage was a glimpse of something extraordinary: whatever happened in David's tabernacle, God wanted to rebuild again. This was not just something that we did, but something God said he would do.

In the eighth century BC the nation of Israel was lost, plunging blindly to its doom. Amos was one of the prophets foretelling the coming devastation, but ended his challenging message to the assembly of Israel with a promise of hope. Something would restore God's presence among his people: the tabernacle of David.

Captivated, I began rapidly thumbing to the cross-reference in Acts 15 where the text is quoted eight hundred years later at the Council in Jerusalem. James was agreeing with Peter, Paul and Barnabas that only belief in Jesus was required for salvation, therefore the new Gentile believers should not be burdened with the Law of Moses. The practice of circumcision was under debate, so I imagine that there was a frank exchange of views!

James stood and quoted from the prophet Amos:

'After this I will return and will rebuild the tabernacle of David, which has fallen down; I will rebuild its ruins, and I will set it up; so that the rest of mankind may seek the Lord, even all the Gentiles who are called by my name,' says the Lord who does all these things. (Acts 15:16–17 NKJV)

God said he would rebuild David's fallen tent so that all people would seek him – not just the nation of Israel, but the whole of humanity. I believe that where places like the tabernacle of David exist, God's presence will be also. God loved David and he wants that special kind of worship to take place again, over and over again, all across the earth!

This declaration rocked my world then and still compels me today. Our Father in heaven promises something in his presence that will bring home the lost, the hurting and broken and begin to transform them for his glory. It will happen in a 'tent' like David's, rebuilt by the hand of the Father in partnership with a passionate people...and then the rest of mankind will seek him.

Corporate worship

Since that time I have believed when God's people gather to worship: not just to sing songs, read words, pray and hear sermons, but to bring the overflowing thankfulness of our hearts, release a prophetic sound, and sing a new song, we will change the spiritual atmosphere. As we honour God, lives will be changed, bodies will be healed, and hearts will be restored.

The aim of this book is to testify to my own experience, putting into context what I saw in these two passages. It is about corporate worship that is unencumbered by a framework or programme, and totally focused on God – Father, Son and Holy Spirit.

When James quoted the prophet Amos, he was showing that the old covenant, which kept Jews and Gentiles separate, was no longer in operation. He was trying to persuade the assembly to agree not to force its laws on the new Gentile believers, because God wants to draw all mankind to him, not just Israel.

Amos and James may not have been thinking of corporate worship, yet God spoke something deep into my heart about restoring a genuine encounter with his people. God says he will do it! And as we look deeper into what happened in David's tent, I hope you may catch that same vision for worship. I hear the call of God for his people and I believe he wants a 'yes' from us in response.

My desire for our church for many, many years is to have 'a place to call home and a place of his presence.' Rather than hiring halls and meeting in schools and social clubs, as we have for over twenty nomadic years, I personally long for our own 'sanctuary' dedicated to his name. As it is filled with a people sold out to pursue his presence, we will see that place become a beacon for the lost, hurting and broken.

The New Covenant promise is not just a place to call home, but for God to call his people home. God is looking for people dedicated to worship and where he finds them, his presence becomes magnificently manifest! It can happen in individual hearts, family homes, coffee shops, teen-lounges, prayer rooms and sanctuaries set aside for seeking him. Burn 24:7 is one growing movement doing this, with groups of likeminded people gathering in many different locations to worship and pray, unifying around their first love.

In his presence is the fullness of joy. (Psalm 16:11)

The promise in his presence is joy...overflowing, life-changing joy! We also know that in his presence is salvation, healing, transformation and so much more than we could possibly ask or imagine. Let me share an example.

Freedom's song

My band and I were at Faith Community Church in Easton, Pennsylvania during a short tour in the USA several years ago. We were all pretty tired due to jet lag and long days of pouring ourselves out at a Tabernacle of David worship conference in the Lehigh Valley. That Sunday evening we were at a meeting hosted by Rev. Patrick Weber. During a time to rest, pray, and gather ourselves before the service started, God's presence filled the room and the joy of the Lord filled us!

We spent quite a while laughing. Laughter is good medicine and it was very refreshing. Patrick's wonderful worship team kicked the evening off, which was good, as our keyboard player Matt was still so full of the joy of the Lord he was in no position to play his keyboard. In Acts 2:15 those who were filled with the Spirit were assumed to be drunk, despite not having had a drop of alcohol, and we all know how inebriated people can behave!

When it was time for our band to start, we dragged Matt into position but he just slumped down behind the keyboards! Not to worry, I thought, the first song is mostly guitars so we'll carry on without him. He became a sign that makes you wonder. I explained what had happened in the prayer room before the service, demonstrating to our American congregation that we Brits aren't so reserved after all!

Matt, bless him, made many attempts to play and quite amazingly played a whole tune from the floor with just his hands reaching up to the keys. I had to try very hard not to laugh hysterically. Then we hit a point during our worship time when I sensed the atmosphere changing and could feel the presence of God filling the place. I knew something was about to happen.

Scripture promises that Jesus will be in our midst when we gather in his name (Matthew 18:20). As the music and spontaneous song continued, I sensed that God's power was present to heal (Luke 5:17), and asked people to stand and place a hand on parts of their body where there was pain. I made a simple decree of healing and blessed those standing. We then waited in his presence.

Then I asked if anyone could sense God at work, and many said their pain was lessened or completely better. One older lady with chronic arthritis had hobbled in earlier with two sticks, but came up positively bouncing. She described how she had suffered over many years and the struggle it was to get to church that night. After a few moments in the presence and a simple decree, her joints were totally healed and she was free to dance and celebrate, which we all did in response to the goodness of God!

As we carried on giving thanks and worshipping there was also a sense of freedom being released, so we called up those needing a fresh touch from the Lord. Many people were in tears. The ministry team prayed for many at the front as the band and I continued to play and sing out over them. I could see many deeply affected, especially a couple of young girls down at the front.

Afterwards the female youth pastor showed me a knife. One of the girls who turned up at church had been depressed and hopeless and was planning to use it to commit suicide later that night. Yet during the worship when she encountered the love of Abba, Daddy God, she was so deeply touched that she gave her heart to Jesus and had a powerful deliverance. I wept as the story unfolded. As she continued to take steps of freedom, the church family took care of her.

Extraordinary things happen when we make space for God to do what he wants in our gatherings. When we hear, obey and flow with God's heart and are led by the Holy Spirit, nothing is impossible. Lives are saved, mind-sets are changed, bodies get healed, and Jesus gets all the glory he deserves.

Vision brings about purpose

Since I first read that passage in Amos, I have believed that this kind of unified worship must be given the priority it deserves. God truly inhabits the praises of his people, and that atmosphere of praise and adoration contains miraculous potential for breakthrough as we encounter his presence. When heaven kisses earth, we get caught in the embrace!

I still have the notes I wrote at the time, with that revelation of his eternal truth. When we worship with our whole heart, the promise from heaven will be released. It is exciting to see it happening increasingly around the world, because God is visibly moving. We get to partner with divine purpose to see his kingdom come in all its fullness!

Rebuild, return, rebuild

I believe God wants to restore our heart's passion for his presence. He wants us to return to him, responding to his promises with joyful anticipation! God is truly good all the time and wants our hearts aligned with his. It's not about striving, but surrender.

David was described as a man after God's heart, because

he loved the things that God did. God took pleasure in David's tent and what went on in it twenty-four hours a day for thirty-three years: the songs, the instruments, the musicians and singers. He loved the worshippers with hearts full of praise and adoration. He delighted that an unknown shepherd from Judah obeyed his call.

David came from the fields to give a prophetic call to worshippers in the future. God so loved David's Tabernacle that he called an unknown shepherd and farmer from Judah to the assembly at Bethel to declare the "Lion's Roar" of God's judgement over Israel and deliver a prophetic call to worshippers in the future. God also inspired James, a younger brother of Jesus, to quote the words of that prophet Amos at a crucial council in Jerusalem to include the Gentiles in on the promise of salvation.

'I will return and rebuild David's fallen tent...' What he did in David's tabernacle, he will do again. '... so that the remnant of men will seek the Lord.'

God draws near

I believe that encounter leads to transformation, in God's glorious timing, from one degree of glory to another. Part of that process is the ongoing renewing of our minds and the way we think. If we worship as David did, God promises that he will be drawn to those people pursuing his presence.

God really does come near to us, closer and closer. So when we gather with hearts overflowing with adoration we are not just performing a religious service, we are passionately worshiping the Creator of all things. That kind of worship is an end in itself.

Combustion

I believe God is searching the earth for those that truly love him. And when we find him, combustion happens – we have a miracle-working God. I believe we are to be 'flammable' ones who are easily set alight. We should all be burning, ignited

PROMISE OF THE PRESENCE

with passion and purpose for the King and his kingdom.

One scripture that resonates for me is: *'His word was in my heart like a burning fire shut up in my bones and I am weary of holding it back and indeed … I cannot!'* (Jeremiah 20:9 NIV).

It's up to us to keep fuelling the flame in the altar of our hearts through our expressions of worship.

Our wholehearted response to the Saviour of our souls releases the promise of heaven. We sing to him who rejoices over us with singing and are drawn to a loving Father who wants an intimate relationship with his children. We are all God's children and he is a really good Dad!

So in the same way that David captured the heart of the Father, we can too. As we draw near to him, he draws near to us.

Healing during worship

In services at my home church Bridge, in Southampton, we have seen many people healed and mightily touched, just during times of worship. One elderly lady in our congregation had been ill with diverticulitis. During a particularly deep time in God's presence she felt heat on her abdomen and the following week she testified that all her symptoms had gone, and didn't return.

In another service a visitor who sat near the aisle was visibly affected during the worship. He was an actor who had travelled to Southampton that day from the US to perform at the Mayflower Theatre for a week. He had been suffering terrible pain in his right knee, had to wear a knee support and could not move his legs freely.

However, as he listened to the testimonies at the start of our meeting he began to think that he could be healed. During the worship he began to bend his knee, and kept doing it. After a while he realised that God had healed him completely! God knew his need and met him during our service. Some of our people prayed with him before he left and he went away with a new understanding of Father God.

Recently I made a simple declaration that I expected people to be healed during worship: no prayers or ministry, just God's glorious presence. After a celebratory time of worship a man came up and said that just after I'd spoken about healing, he tested his body out. He had suffered severe pain and limited movement, but all his pain was now gone. This happened before we played a note, just in anticipation of a good Dad doing something good for his kids!

I love to see people getting lost in the warm embrace of the Father during worship. They end up on their knees or on their faces before him as they are overwhelmed by his love. God is transforming us from one glory to another through wonderful encounters and it is so exciting and humbling to be part of that.

Kids see angelic activity, young people find passion, and all ages wonderfully enjoy the intensity of God's presence. My elderly mother-in-law, May, used to love worshipping with her eyes closed and head back, doing her little Granny dance. It is beautiful to witness these personal, intimate encounters. The invitation is there for all of us; it's not age-dependent, just heart-dependent.

I believe there is no limit to what God can and will do in the atmosphere of abandoned worship. In the presence of his glory is salvation, healing and deliverance – nothing is impossible. Even before the preacher stands up, even before an appeal or an altar call, God's wonderful Spirit will deliver the bounty of heaven to searching and purposeful hearts.

If you build it...

The film called 'Field of Dreams' is about a struggling Iowa farmer with a crazy passion for baseball. He hears the whisper of a cryptic message: 'If you build it...he will come.' Although he tries to ignore it, that message doesn't leave him alone and he catches a vision of something beyond his understanding. Despite ridicule and opposition he spends money he can scarce afford to build a baseball diamond in his cornfield in the middle of nowhere.

As the story develops Shoeless Joe Jackson and other baseball legends of the Chicago White Sox come to play once again and the word spreads. At the end of the movie a line of cars is disappearing off into the horizon, full of people coming to watch the amazing spectacle in his field of dreams. All his life this man has been searching for his dreams but in the end his dreams come and find him. Though it's a fantasy story, I have found that eternal truths often embed themselves in contemporary culture.

For me it's a prophetic echo of God's heart in Amos 9 and Acts 15. The screenplay says 'If you build it, they will come.' God says, 'I will return and rebuild David's fallen tent, so that the remnant of men will seek the Lord.' The offer is open to the world, to all of mankind. He will rebuild it so that you and I will seek him!

So we just need to respond. If we turn our affections towards him, then I believe God will appear in greater measure than we can imagine. We must choose to make room for the Holy Spirit and invite him to take control. If we love him more than our programs, our plans and our liturgy, and dedicate ourselves to worship him with all our mind, heart and strength, his presence will come!

Like the Iowa farmer hearing 'the voice,' I felt the shepherd's voice calling to me. My heart was intent to pursue this glorious promise to us to drink and be refreshed, to seek out meaning and purpose for our lives, to be re-charged and invigorated, as we host the presence of God.

Beacon for the lost

Many times since then, I've partaken of and had the privilege to lead this kind of worship that I saw in my vision. Once experienced, there is a healthy dissatisfaction with anything less than the best. God deserves the best we have, as he has given us the best of heaven.

Not only is the Father's house a place of refreshing,

renewal and transformation, but it is also a guiding light in the darkness. It is a beacon for the lost and the broken who will find what they have been searching for all their lives, a loving relationship with their heavenly Father. Jesus called him Abba – literally, Daddy – and God wants you to know him in this intimate way too.

At one of our Sunday services not long after my revelation in Amos, a few young people who had been attending our services brought some rowdy lads along who were making fun of us 'happy-clappy' Christians gathered in a school hall. We carried on praising God despite the ruckus in the back of the room, and then suddenly something changed.

I do like the 'and suddenly's' of God (Malachi 3:1). The Lord suddenly appeared to those sceptical young people. One lad came to the front and apologized for planning to mess up the meeting. He said that during the worship he met with God and felt his love, a real, warming love unlike anything he had experienced before, and it had overwhelmed him.

This young man wanted to make a commitment to Jesus. There was no preaching, just the wonderful presence of the Father touching a troubled heart and setting it free. He left with a big smile on his face and my Bible in his hand!

Healing and salvation

Many years later, in Columbia with Randy Clark on a Global Awakening trip, I experienced the wonderfully exuberant praise of the passionate people in its second largest city, Medellin. The presence of God was so thick. Before and after the meetings the international ministry team prayed for the sick, especially those with terminal conditions, in wheelchairs, or walking with crutches.

In one meeting there was an uproar of celebration. One woman displayed her medical records while joyfully testifying to healing of all the pain of the cancer in her body. Several people launched themselves across the stage holding aloft their crutches and walking sticks to the shouts and cheers of the congregation. We laid hands on one young lad who was deaf and dumb from birth, the deaf and dumb spirit left him, and he began to hear and then speak for the first time!

It was stunning to see so many miracles in this converted warehouse, all in an atmosphere of worship and adoration. When Randy preached the good news that night, literally hundreds of people ran to the altar to give their lives to Jesus! Truly, everyone who calls on the name of the Lord will be saved.

The search of the hungry

In the vision God gave me, as the whole church caught the vision in unity, people were drawn in to the presence. I read that after the tragedy of 9/11, many New Yorkers flooded into churches seeking solace and comfort, yet most drifted away eventually because they didn't find what they were looking for. They came because they were hungry, but they left because there was nothing to eat. People are looking for something real and fulfilling.

When Jesus delivered a man possessed by an impure spirit at the Capernaum synagogue (Mark 1:21-34), by sunset people from the whole town had camped outside Simon and Andrew's doorstep, bringing their sick and demon-possessed to be healed. If there is genuine substance to what we profess, people will not just come, they may well dig a hole in the roof to get in!

The Great Commission tells us to 'go', so we don't expect everyone to walk over our threshold. But there is a need for a place that people can come to and belong to, because people need family.

Bread on the table

In the temple in Jerusalem there was showbread on a dedicated table – a pile of bread or cake. In Hebrew it literally means 'the bread of the presence.' (Cake in the temple – church welcome teams, take note!) It was always kept fresh by the priests.

There should be bread in the house of God because the hungry are searching for real, fresh bread, not stale crumbs. The thirsty are looking for living, refreshing water and they need to find it in our gatherings. When the Father's house is filled with his love, the prodigals will come home.

'Blessed are those who hunger and thirst for righteousness for they shall be filled.' (Matthew 5:6 NIV)

God greatly desires to satisfy our hunger for him and his ways. In Acts 13:52 we read how the disciples were continually filled with joy and with the Holy Spirit. Moses prayed, 'Let me know your ways that I may know you,' and David sang, 'When I see you face to face I will be satisfied.' Jesus promised that as we hunger for God and his ways, we shall be filled.

Jesus declares the blessing of heaven, saying, 'I will fill you with all the fullness of the Father, and when you drink from me, rivers of living waters will flow from inside of you!' The 'desire of the nations' (Haggai 2:7) is living in us, giving us hope. And the joy of the Lord is our strength, in all situations and circumstances.

Believe it or not, the world is hungry for what we have. People have an aching yearning to be loved and released into a life of destiny and purpose. We have the answer, Christ in us, the hope of glory! When we live in the presence of the all-sufficient one, we have all we need, and more to give away.

In his presence

Moses, who was marked by every face-to-face encounter he had with God, knew the importance of his presence. He pleaded with the Lord, *'do not send me out without your presence because what else will distinguish us from everyone else?'* (Exodus 33:15). Moses was unwilling to leave that place without the promise of God's presence surrounding him.

Joshua would not depart from the tent of meeting after Moses had returned to the camp (Exodus 33:10-11). This is the man who took Israel into the Promised Land in three days after they had delayed for forty years. He loved to linger in the presence of God, and ultimately was used by God to fulfil the promise over his people.

David too pleaded with God not to take his presence from him (Psalm 51:5). For David the Holy Spirit was precious, joy bringing, and life giving. It meant safety and shelter and satisfaction. He described his great longing: 'One thing have I desired, to dwell in the house of the Lord all the days of my life' (Psalm 27:4).

David wanted to live under God's instruction and guidance, protection and provision, where he could find answers as he enquired of the Lord. God defines us and he refines us too. He will maintain us in the midst of seeming chaos and order our lives for his glory.

David's chief desire was to live in the constant and consistent presence of God: *'Surely your goodness and love will follow me all the days of my life, and I will dwell in the house of the Lord forever'* (Psalm 23:6 NIV). Oh, for an encounter with this wonderful presence. Once we are captivated by the love of the Father, nothing else in the world will satisfy.

David was truly a man with a heart after God. He longed for 'one thing' and realised that God longs for that with us, as the scriptures reiterate – 'Return to me' (Joel 2:12)...'come to me' (Matt 11:28)...'draw near to me and I will draw near to you' (James 4:8)

This is the promise of the Father to his children, from the loved to the beloved. He rewards those who seek him (Hebrews 11:6) and wants us to have the same passion as David did to know him and abide with him. David found in his tabernacle something so profound and so precious that everything else dimmed into insignificance. And because of this priority Israel knew peace and prosperity not seen before in their history. The favour of the Lord rested on not just a man, or a city, but on a nation.

2

THE TABERNACLE OF DAVID

There were two remarkable buildings in the Old Testament – the tabernacle of Moses and the temple of Solomon. Both were designed and inspired by God to host his presence, in the form of the Ark of the Covenant. They were a dwelling place for his name.

God himself was the architect of the tabernacle of Moses as he came down on Mount Sinai in thunder and lightning. Moses stood hidden in the storm cloud of God's glory for forty days while the Lord laid out detailed plans for the holy place, the altar for sacrifice and the holy of holies concealing the Ark of the Covenant. That tabernacle became the place of worship for Israel throughout the wilderness (Exodus 24-31).

In a sense what Moses began in the wilderness, Solomon finished in the Promised Land. He built an extraordinary temple for the Lord, with his father David's provision and designs (1 Chronicles 28 and 29). Scholars calculate that it was the most expensive building per square metre ever built, somewhere in the in the region of $140 billion! That shows how extraordinarily prosperous God's people were following King David's reign.

Yet God didn't say through Amos, 'I will return and rebuild the Temple of Solomon,' or, 'I will restore the ruins of the Tabernacle of Moses...' No, he said:

'I will raise up the tent of David, which has fallen down, and

repair its damages. I will raise up its ruins, and rebuild it as in the days of old, that they may possess the remnant of Edom, and all the Gentiles who are called by my name,' says the Lord who does this thing. (Amos 9:11–12 NKJV)

Neither the divinely designed tabernacle of Moses, nor the skilled, extravagant craftsmanship of the temple of Solomon were chosen. God says he will raise up again the tabernacle of David, something barely described in scripture:

'...he [David] prepared a place for the ark of God and pitched a tent for it.' (1 Chronicles 15:1 NIV)

That's it! That is all there is written about the structure of David's tent in Scripture. David got out his mallet and pitched a tent for the Ark. No mention of the type of wood for the tent poles, the fabric used for the walls and roof, the dimensions and scale... David's priority was simply to host the manifest presence of God. What was it about David's tent that God saw as so special?

Old Testament worship was governed by a complex system of rules and regulations to show that God is holy and the people were not. There were offerings of various shapes, sizes and smells, to atone for just about every eventuality.

Yet not only did David replace God's covenantal instructions for worship with an idea of his own, through Amos' prophecy, but God appeared to use this as shorthand for his plans of restoration. But what is God intending to restore? And what happened in David's tent that made God hold it up as a blueprint for his people in the generations to come?

Not just the restoration of a nation

'After this I will return and rebuild David's fallen tent. Its ruins I will rebuild, and I will restore it, that the rest of mankind may seek the Lord, even all the Gentiles who bear my name,' says the Lord, who does these things—things known from long ago. (Acts 15:16-18 NIV)

So we had the tabernacle of Moses designed by God, the tabernacle of David pitched by the king and then a third 'tabernacle' – its restoration. But, before our camera zooms in to focus on David's tent, let's take a brief panoramic view of salvation history, to understand Amos' words.

After Solomon's death in 922 BC, his empire collapsed virtually overnight. This left two smaller states, Israel and Judah, fighting for survival against hostile neighbours and even each other. However, by the middle of the eighth century BC, the regional superpower Assyria was weakened by conflicts both internally and outside its borders.

Under the able leadership of Jeroboam II of Israel (786-746 BC) and Uzziah of Judah (783-742 BC), the states combined to control an area almost as big as Solomon's empire once again. However, despite this resurgence, all was not well. Assyria, Egypt and Babylon would rise as threats over the next two centuries. And Israel and Judah were in severe breach of their covenant obligations, on which God's protection and blessing depended (see Deuteronomy 27-30).

Into this atmosphere of outward prosperity but inward decay, God sent the 'latter prophets' to call his people back to their spiritual heritage or face destruction and exile. Amos was the first of these prophets to appear, around 760 BC.

Neither state responded adequately and Israel was wiped off the map by Assyria in 722 BC and Judah exiled to Babylon in 586 BC. Since the latter prophets spoke over a period of three centuries, before, during and after these events, we must not over-generalise their message. But many of them foresaw some sort of restoration after the necessary judgement, as Amos did, envisioning the united Davidic kingdom with unparalleled security and fertility in the land.

However, half a millennium later, this had still not taken place. Judah's return from exile to Jerusalem in 538 BC was only under Persian occupation following their defeat of the Babylonians. The Greeks succeeded the Persians in 334 BC but, while the Jews managed to oust them in 164 BC, they only succeeded in maintaining a fragile independence until the ascendant Romans rolled in to occupy Jerusalem in 63 BC.

For hundreds of years the prophets of the Lord were silent. During those lean centuries of unfulfilled hopes, Jewish expectations of the coming Messiah became skewed. They now looked for a warrior king leading them to freedom, rather than the 'Prince of Peace' leading them to the Father.

But Jesus exploded these hopes. He didn't act to end the Roman occupation, and he prophesied the destruction of everything seen as central to the restoration, namely Jerusalem and its temple (Mark 13), which occurred in 70 AD. Yet through the cross, he brought into being an altogether greater, eternal kingdom in which all of creation will be redeemed and reconciled (Colossians 1:15-20), not just Israel.

One sign of that kingdom's inauguration was the uniting of Jews and Gentiles as one in Christ. This happened through the removal of the old covenant which had previously separated them (Ephesians 2:13-16). When James recognised this, having heard the apostles' testimony at the Council in Jerusalem in 49 AD, he cited Amos' prophecy as evidence that it was in accord with the Scriptures. In Christ all nations could have access to the covenant relationship with God.

Jesus taught that the Old Testament pointed to him (Luke 24:25-27; John 5:39-40, 45-47). He fulfilled Israel's commission to be a blessing to the nations (Genesis 12:1-3), and we, his followers, now live to reconcile everyone to him (2 Corinthians 5:16-21). This was the biblical touch paper that God lit to explode a passion for worship in me as a young man.

Now, we can easily see Jesus as the promised king who restores the rule of David. But why describe it as the restoration of David's tent? Usually, the words David's house (1 Kings 12:20; Isaiah 7:13; Luke 2:4) and throne (1 Kings 2:45; Jeremiah 17:125; Luke 1:32) are used, or David's kingdom, reign, line, dynasty and family. Amos could have used any one of these words, but somehow God inspired him to use the language of David's tent being restored.

My journey into the promise of the presence has been inspired by the life of David as a worshipper and what took place in his tent in Jerusalem. I really believe that there is something about it that God is restoring in the new covenant here and now. So what is the tabernacle of David?

2 Samuel and 1 and 2 Chronicles show us that the tabernacle of David was a tent that David erected on Mount Zion in Jerusalem in which he placed the ark – the symbol of God's presence (2 Samuel 6:17). David reigned over all Israel for thirty-three years (2 Samuel 5:4-5) and the ark remained in the tent until the temple was built a year or so before his death (1 Chronicles 6:31-32).

Priests and musicians were appointed to commemorate, to thank and praise God before the ark (1 Chronicles 16:4). This happened every day (1 Chronicles 16:37) and probably round the clock as it certainly was in the temple (1 Chronicles 9:33). After David's death the pattern he established continued in the temple during Solomon's reign (2 Chronicles 5-7) and was periodically resurrected by God-fearing kings.

So what was so good and significant about what happened in that tent during those thirty-three years, that God wants to restore it in these last days?

A people after God's own heart

What went on in David's tent had a lot to do with the character of David. This brilliant but flawed, multi-faceted man was a shepherd, a giant-slayer, an adulterer and murderer, a charismatic leader, a warrior king, a prophet, and a worshipper. But for me, one phrase stands out that sums David up best of all, as Samuel spoke about him to Saul:

'...the Lord has sought out a man after his own heart and appointed him leader of his people.' (1 Samuel 13:14 NIV)

When we say, 'There's a man after my own heart,' we usually mean, 'That is someone who loves what I love, and does what I would do.' When God says this, it has an even deeper meaning. As the lover pursues the beloved with passionate intensity and total commitment to win the beloved's heart, so David pursued God. He loved God and loved what God loved, and perhaps for that single quality God promised his family line would rule forever (2 Samuel 17:13-16).

For all time Jesus is described as the 'Son of David,' from the line of David (Matthew 1:1), even while he is now ruling and reigning in the heavens as King of kings, the Alpha and Omega, and the Lord of lords! What an incredible legacy. God stays true to his promise and word, and it is sometimes beyond our limited understanding.

The Bible regards the heart as the executive centre of the self. As the boss, it draws together every spiritual process, thinks, feels and moralises, takes responsibility and directs the will. So to have the heart is to have the whole person. God clearly had all of David because God had David's heart. God wants our hearts too! He wants a people after his own heart and a people who love what he loves.

A people wanting to praise him

When we come into the presence of our God who is infinite, unchanging, all-knowing, omnipresent, all-powerful, righteous, just, true, loving, merciful and totally committed to us, how do we respond? We can only do as the four living creatures do eternally before his throne:

Day and night they never stop saying: 'Holy, holy, holy is the Lord God Almighty, who was, and is, and is to come.' Whenever the living creatures give glory, honour and thanks to him who sits on the throne and who lives for ever and ever, the twenty-four elders fall down before him who sits on the throne, and worship him who lives for ever and ever. They lay their crowns before the throne and say: *'You are worthy, our Lord and God, to receive glory and honour and power, for you created all things, and by your will they were created and have their being.'* (Revelation 4:8-11 NIV)

Here and now we can start what we will be doing forever. Worship though, is not limited to singing songs; it is the way we live our lives.

David created a plan for wholehearted music, singing, prophesying, movement and dancing in praise to God in his tent. He made the animal sacrifices and offerings that God required to atone for sin (2 Samuel 6:17), but he also spoke of the sacrifices of joy (Psalm 27:6), thanksgiving (Psalm 50:8-15), brokenness (Psalm 51:16-17), praise (Psalm 54:6) and prayer (Psalm 141:2).

If we love someone we will do anything for them, and if we really want to do something we will find a way. David was prepared to give everything in worship. He lost the respect of his wife for his 'undignified' leaping and dancing before God (2 Samuel 6:16). He regarded worship that cost him nothing as no worship at all (2 Samuel 24:18-25).

The New Testament also speaks of worship and life in sacrificial terms (Hebrews 13:15-16). If wholehearted, undignified praise is too much trouble for us, then we have to question how much we really love God. For I believe God is looking for a people after his own heart, 'a people wanting to praise him.'

A people wanting to please him

David was a man full of the Spirit of God (1 Samuel 16:12), zealous for God's cause (1 Samuel 17:45-47) obedient to God's plans (1 Samuel 26:9-11) and walking in God's ways (1 Kings 3:14).

The heart of the true worshipper hungers for more of the Eternal One and desires to live humbly before him in vulnerability and authenticity. Doing all we do unto the Lord is worship.

The type of worship that went on in David's tent exemplifies what God regards as most important of all:

'Love the Lord your God with all your heart and with all your soul and with all your mind.' This is the first and greatest commandment. And the second is like it: 'Love your neighbour as yourself.' All the Law and the Prophets hang on these two commandments. (Matthew 22:37-40 NIV)

Jesus gave this command to call out the champion heart in each one of us to go after all who God is with everything we are. And we show our love for God by the way we love one another. How we treat each other is as much a measure of our love for God as how we treat him! When love is expressed unconditionally, then God is worshipped.

We are made in his image and inhabited by his Spirit. If he is contained within each one of us, how can we say we love him when we mistreat what looks like him? Jesus said 'When you do it to the least you have done it to me.'

'Truly I say to you, to the extent that you did it to one of these brothers of mine, even the least of them, you did it to me.' (Matthew 25:40 NASB)

That is why Jesus told us to quickly deal with grievances:

Therefore if you bring your gift to the altar, and there remember that your brother has something against you, leave your gift there before the altar, and go your way. First be reconciled to your brother, and then come and offer your gift. (Matthew 5:23-24 NKJV)

Notice how we are responsible for doing the restoration. I greatly value my relationships and sometimes that means I have to go low. Godly authority in our lives only comes when we walk in humility and maturity; otherwise we can end up controlling instead of loving those around us.

God called his creation very good (Genesis 1:31). If Jesus didn't separate the first and second commandments, neither should we. God wants a people that love him, and also love what he loves, with everything they can muster.

David's hunger for the presence of God touched my heart powerfully and pulled me to pursue God with the same kind of passion. So I pour myself out, giving him everything I have, making a sacrifice of praise to be sweet incense consumed by fire. I'm not going to leave it for the rocks to cry out – I have a voice and I intend to raise it again and again in adoration of my faithful Father. I hope this inspires and encourages others to do the same.

David discipled other musicians, and had his chief musicians apprentice and train others. Over the years I've walked alongside passionate worshippers, encouraging budding songwriters, facilitating worship and releasing many into roles of leadership. David's tent was a spiritual powerhouse that enabled a nation to live in unprecedented peace – and God is restoring it all over the earth.

3

A MAN AFTER GOD'S HEART

King David's prodigious passion and vision had an impact on all of history and still affects us now, through God's promise over his life. But how did he get from hillside shepherd boy to conquering king with peace on all sides? Many great books have already studied David's life, but let's discover more about how he pursued God's presence.

David the shepherd boy

Somewhere in between the tabernacle of Moses and the temple of Solomon, there was a young shepherd boy singing alone on a hillside. While guarding the family herd of sheep, he sang passionate songs of worship written out of the overflow of his heart to an audience of one. Those songs stirred heaven and showed us what God was longing for in his people.

David was the youngest of eight sons, overlooked by his family, who left him alone tending the sheep. When the prophet Samuel visited Jesse's home to meet his sons, no one even bothered to call David into the house! But David was not overlooked by the Almighty. He was chosen and anointed by God. He didn't look the part, unlike Saul, who was head and shoulders above the rest. Saul was a man's man, you might say, but David was God's man.

So Samuel took the horn of oil and anointed him in the presence of his brothers, and from that day on the Spirit of the Lord came powerfully upon David. (1 Samuel16:13, NIV)

Out in the fields David must have discovered things about himself and about his God. He learned to listen, to worship, and to fight. Away from public gaze he slew the bear and the lion rather than give up one of his flock. He had great courage because he knew who his Almighty God was. He would not have the wild animals steal his family's sheep. And he would not hear the armies of the living God being insulted by a Philistine (1 Samuel 17).

David the warrior

While the army of Israel quivered in their boots, David got indignant. Anointed by the Spirit of the Lord and with the prophetic decree of Samuel still resonating in his ear, he stepped onto the battlefield full of courage and confidence. His passion was prodigious. He wasn't swayed by his brothers' angry advice to go back home to his sheep or dissuaded by King Saul, who tried to put him off: 'the youth is surely no match for a trained man of war?'

David would not relent. Instead of the king's ill-fitting armour, he clothed himself in the righteousness of God. He also decreed what was to take place, prophesying the outcome of the fight before he even stepped foot on the battlefield (1 Samuel 17:45–47).

There is power in announcing what is going to happen before it happens. Like our spiritual father Abraham, we need to place our trust in God's version of reality more than our apparent circumstances and speak that which is not, as though it is (Romans 4:17). Faith comes from hearing (Romans 10:17)! When we speak we listen, so when we speak out God's version of reality, it has an impact on our expectation and understanding. It raises our faith.

Jesus said that he spoke and acted on the basis of what his Father gave him to see, hear and know (John 5:19-20,

30;12:48-50). Surely this also applies to those born-again with his Spirit and called to represent him on the earth. When we declare on earth a promise made in heaven, then heaven does indeed come to earth!

David's decree before the battle with Goliath reminds me of the movie scene when 'Gladiator' stands on the blood-spattered dust of the Coliseum's arena of death, surrounded by the threatening spear points of the Royal Guard. Facing his nemesis, the emperor, he slowly removes the helmet covering his face and declares his true identity and his position of authority:

My name is Maximus Decimus Meridius, commander of the armies of the North, general of the Felix Legions, loyal servant to the true emperor Marcus Aurelius, father to a murdered son, husband to a murdered wife, and I will have my vengeance in this life or the next!

It's stirring stuff indeed...

On a battlefield in the Elah Valley a shepherd boy stood before the might of Philistine army and one giant of a man. The roar of the soldiers must have died down to a whisper as he stood on the edge of the battlefield to deliver his speech...

David said to the Philistine, *'You come against me with sword and spear and javelin, but I come against you in the name of the Lord Almighty, the God of the armies of Israel, whom you have defied. This day the Lord will hand you over to me, and I'll strike you down and cut off your head. Today I will give the carcasses of the Philistine army to the birds of the air and the beasts of the earth, and the whole world will know that there is a God in Israel. All those gathered here will know that it is not by sword or spear that the Lord saves; for the battle is the Lord's, and he will give all of you into our hands.'* (1 Samuel 17:45–47 NIV)

David ran at the Philistine army and directly at Goliath. Using his tried and tested sling, he took a stone destined from the beginning of creation to make its mark on history, and on one particular forehead. The pebble from the brook left David's hand with the force of heaven behind it. With the same courage with which he tackled a lion, he faced up to a giant, before two warring armies. He would honour the name of the Lord whoever was watching.

As soon as Goliath's body hit the ground, David's life changed forever. He routed the Philistine army and everything he had prophetically decreed beforehand came about. This brought him to the king's attention and a deep friendship with the king's son Jonathan, another courageous man. David went from a hillside camp to a kingly household overnight.

Years later when David himself became king of Israel he ousted the Philistines who were once again occupying his territory and captured the Canaanite enclave of Jerusalem (2 Samuel 1-5). In doing so he completed the invasion of the Promised Land that Joshua began, thus giving him a neutral city from which to rule and unify the tribes of Israel.

Wanting his presence

The Psalms clearly show how David wanted to live in the presence of God. One of his first acts when he became king of all Israel was to retrieve the Ark of the Covenant, also known as the Ark of Agreement – the symbol of God's presence and authority. He was a worshipper.

The journey of the Ark

Upon entering the Promised Land, the tabernacle of Moses was settled at Shiloh in Samaria and stayed there for about 400 years. In a battle with the Philistines at Aphek during Eli's time, the Ark was brought into battle in a last-ditch effort for victory. But the Lord was angry with Israel and they were defeated, becoming 'Ichabod' which means 'no glory.' The Ark was captured and the Philistines occupied part of the land (1 Samuel 4). The tabernacle of Moses in Shiloh was then without the Ark and the glory of his presence.

The Philistines carried the Ark to Ashdod and placed it in the temple of their god, Dagon (1 Samuel 5), but paid dearly for this. The statue of Dagon tumbled face downwards on the ground before the ark, and was broken into pieces. The people suffered with plagues and sent the ark to another Philistine city, Gath, but they suffered horribly with tumours so they also sent it on. Before it even arrived in the next city, Ekron, the people cried out in fear of their lives and they had great troubles too. The Philistines had had enough. After just seven months they returned the ark to Israel in a cart with a payment of symbolic sin offerings cast in gold (1 Samuel 6).

The Ark finally arrived eight miles west of Jerusalem to an obscure town called Kiriath Jearim. The powerful and holy symbol of God's presence remained neglected until David decided to retrieve it. Until then, it appears that no one cared enough to restore the ark to the tabernacle of Moses on Mount Gibeon.

What was the spiritual state of the nation at that time? For decades the Holy of Holies remained empty. What was going on in that tabernacle without the ark? Yes, the priests continued to offer their daily sacrifices and go through their religious rituals, but all without his glory! All without the presence of God in the house of God. Yet the Ark was in a farmhouse just a few miles away.

Reality check

It is sobering to note that religious activity can continue without God's presence being any part of it! Our gatherings should be known for the joyful celebration of the goodness of God, because in his presence is fullness of joy (Psalm 16:11). So in his presence something happens that changes us from the inside out.

We don't gather on a Sunday to go through the motions of a religious service, we gather to joyfully celebrate the glorious King, our personal Saviour, deliverer and healer – Jesus. We have been destined to spend the rest of our lives in his presence!

We are not just mouthing empty words when we pray 'Let your kingdom come, let your will be done, on earth as it is in heaven.' This is a passionate decree, inviting all that is part of heaven to establish itself here on earth. We do that by honouring and hosting the manifest presence of God, and that starts on the inside of us.

King David declared his intent in Psalm 132:

'I will not go home to my house, or lie down on my bed, or close my eyes, or let myself sleep until I find a place for the Lord. I want to provide a home for the mighty God of Jacob.' (Psalm 132:2-5 NCV).

David wanted God's presence in his nation and claimed the ark back for his people. Significantly, in David's tent, the ark was not hidden behind a curtain, as it was in Moses' tent and later in the temple of Solomon, where only the high priest could enter once a year.

On the Day of Atonement, the high priest made meticulous preparations. He had to cleanse himself, put on special clothing, carry burning incense so that the smoke would shield his eyes from a direct view of God, and bring blood to make atonement for sins. A rope was tied around him so that in the event he died, he could be dragged out. The High Priest wasn't supposed to even sweat! That act of service was performed with great reverence and very real holy fear.

He is holy

People died when they looked into the ark (1 Samuel 6:19)! For the villagers to whom the ark had just been returned, it was a life or death experience of the awesome holiness of God. He is the refiner's fire purifying his priests like gold and silver.

David learned this the hard way when he first tried to transport the ark back to Jerusalem. As the ox-drawn cart bumped along the track, Uzzah, one of the helpers, reached out his hand to steady the Ark and was struck down dead for touching it. In their enthusiasm they had forgotten reverence.

The fear of the Lord is the beginning of wisdom, and knowledge of the Holy One is understanding. (Proverbs 9:10 NIV)

Angry and troubled, David left the ark at Obed-Edom's house for some three months. Obed and his household were extremely blessed (2 Samuel 6, 1 Chronicles 15)! David, gaining a healthy respect for the holiness of the Lord, returned to Jerusalem. There he gleaned the understanding he needed to fulfil his desire to see the presence of God restored.

So David reappointed the Levites (1 Chronicles 15) to their original roles to ceremonially return the ark to Jerusalem. They did it with exuberant singing and shouting, playing musical instruments, sounding the shofar and trumpets and bashing bronze cymbals as he led them with passionate dancing. Countless burnt offerings were made before and after the ark was brought inside the tent. Then David blessed the people and gave them gifts of bread and cake.

And so the presence of God was established at the heart of David's rule and re-established at the heart of the nation.

One person who didn't join in that celebration was Michal, David's wife and Saul's daughter. She watched her husband from her window and when she saw him prancing around she despised his extravagant worship in her heart (1 Chronicles 15:29, 2 Samuel 6:20-23). What better day was there for David to celebrate and give all that he had to the Lord than the day the Ark of the Covenant came back into the city? But Michal's response was contempt.

This is reflected in a 'religious spirit' seeking to control and dial down freedom of expression or in political correctness that will reject extravagant acts of worship. The result for Michal was barrenness, and when we judge, despise or try to control others' expressions of worship in our own gatherings it can bring about barrenness.

God's presence restored among his people

There is a prophetic call in worship to respond to the Lord. The golden thread of God's plan woven throughout the tapestry of scripture is his desire to be with his sons and daughters, and for his children to desire to be with him. We are a holy nation, a royal priesthood, a kingdom of priests and a people chosen by God to be his very own.

It was so in the beginning with Adam and Eve (Genesis 3:8-9). It was the invitation to the nation of Israel when Moses was on Mount Sinai (Exodus 19:6). That invitation was confirmed in Peter's first epistle (1 Peter 2:9). And it will be so at the end in the New Jerusalem (Revelation 21:3).

The curtain is torn

When Jesus cried out from the cross, 'It is finished,' the massive, heavy curtain sealing off the holy of holies in the temple was ripped from top to bottom. From now on there would be no separation between God and his people. Jesus' life, death, resurrection and ascension have made the presence of God accessible to everyone without any intermediaries.

Nothing bars us from his glorious presence apart from our willingness to draw near. We can boldly approach the throne of grace (Hebrews 4:16) and not die! We can look upon his face and we can enter into his glorious presence. David's tent was a foretaste of this place where God and his people could meet heart-to-heart, which one day Jesus, the Son of David, would fulfil, so that *'the remnant of men may seek the Lord, and all the Gentiles who bear my name...'* (Acts 15:17 NIV).

His presence is restored
The restoration confirmed at the council of Jerusalem

The year: 49AD. The place: Jerusalem. The people: the assembly of the young mother church, still seen only as an extreme sect of Judaism. And a big question hangs in the air: 'Should the new Gentile believers have to keep the Law of Moses to be saved?' Or to put it bluntly, 'Do the new converts have to be circumcised to be saved?'

For the 'ayes': the many converts from the party of the

Pharisees. God's people were historically Jewish; their Messiah was Jewish; he upheld Moses; so yes of course, get the knife out! For the 'nays:' Paul and Barnabas just returned from their first missionary journey into Asia Minor which saw many miracles, signs and wonders and many converts among the Gentiles.

The apostles and elders retired privately to consider how this issue could be resolved. After much deliberation, Peter threw his lot in with the 'nays.' Seeing the Holy Spirit fall on the centurion Cornelius and his family when they believed his message about Jesus (Acts 10), convinced him that salvation not about obedience to a burdensome ceremonial law. And eating together, so important culturally, was crucial to them being unified as one church. They concluded that people should not have to jump through hoops to belong to the family!

James, their leader, agreed, quoting from scripture:

'After this I will return and rebuild David's fallen tent. Its ruins I will rebuild, and I will restore it, that the remnant of men may seek the Lord, and all the Gentiles who bear my name,' says the Lord, who does these things. (Acts 15:16-17 NIV)

This was a deeply significant day in the church's history, a big step on the journey that would ultimately lead to its separation from Judaism, when it ruled that salvation was no longer confined to the land of Israel and the Law of Moses, and that God's plan was to gather his people from all nations through the restoration of the tent of David.

It seems that David's tent is about calling people to seek God. It is about the establishment of a place of his presence, which God says he will do so all the nations may seek him, including the many outsiders who have been called by his name. But how?

His presence in people

Jesus had no PR team, news service or website. He didn't Tweet, use Facebook or the latest social media app. Yet, everywhere he went, word spread quickly and people came to see him, to hear him, to be healed.

They sought out Jesus in their thousands. Why? Because the presence of the King equals the presence of the kingdom. Jesus lived in, and from, the kingdom of God. The kingdom of heaven is only manifested where the King is manifested and that is primarily in his people.

In God's kingdom there is no evil, only goodness, so Jesus removed evil spirits (Matthew 8:16). There is no sickness, only health, so Jesus healed people (Matthew 4:23-24). There is no need, only abundance, so Jesus fed people (Matthew 14:15-21). There is no exclusion, only acceptance, so Jesus loved people (Matthew 9:10-13).

Everyone is looking for goodness, health, abundance and acceptance. The problem is that they do not routinely see these things in the church and so go looking elsewhere for them. Our marketing activities and events may cause people to seek our church for a while, but only the presence of God causes people to seek him.

The real thing

These days I see people searching for what is genuine. Certainly not the kind of 'genuine' TAG Heuer watch I was offered in a souk in Dubai! I did eventually buy a fake TAG, which if you didn't look too closely might have passed for the genuine article. But the first time I bumped it, the second hand fell off and the lacquer chipped. It wasn't the real thing and ultimately it was disappointing.

I don't think people are looking to be entertained as much as encountered. They are not just seeking something friendly and seeker-sensitive; they are seeking the friend of friends. Although my personal focus is the corporate gathering, the manifest presence of God is so much more than that.

Now it happened on a certain day, as he was teaching, that there were Pharisees and teachers of the law sitting by, who had come out of every town of Galilee, Judea, and Jerusalem. And the power of the Lord was present to heal them. (Luke 5:17, NKJV)

Jesus didn't spend his whole life in a synagogue. He brought heaven down to earth in everyday situations wherever he went. And where his presence is, so is his power to heal.

My wife and I are involved in is HOTS – Healing on the Streets. The teams go to where people are, rather than expecting them to attend a service, and invite them to stop for a few moments to receive prayer for their needs. With a simple prayer of command we have seen peace come, pain leave, ulcers disappear, headaches go instantly and demonic stuff cast out... just outside Sainsbury's!

Mark Marx, founder of HOTS writes:

We create a thin place on the streets where heaven and earth meet; an environment that's spiritually rich – a spiritual oasis where stillness falls, full of the presence and power of the Holy Spirit. This gentle ministry works within a loving and compassionate environment, full of the presence and power of the Holy Spirit.

The presence is the gathering point for the ministry of the authentic gospel of Jesus.

The promise of his presence restored

There was something very precious about David's tent that God wants for all time, for his people called by his name. David pulled something into his day which was destined for the new covenant. He brought in a new order of authentic and exuberant worship, far removed from the solemn ceremony of Moses' tabernacle. It was wholehearted, physical worship in God's presence.

We need to understand the profound significance of David's heart after God. David was a forerunner, doing something ahead of his time that wasn't supposed to happen until the Holy Spirit fell at Pentecost.

In the tabernacle of Moses there was an outer court and furnishings, but in the tabernacle of David there was nothing apart from the golden Ark of the Covenant, resting on the mercy seat between the cherubim. In the tabernacle of Moses there was a furnished holy place, but in David's tabernacle there was no separate holy place – it was a holy place.

In the tabernacle of Moses there was a Holy of Holies which the High Priest only entered once a year. Yet in David's simple tent there was no thick temple curtain to protect them from his glory. The priests, the singers and musicians came in every day, and stayed there all day, working in one-hour shifts to present worship around the clock. There were no bowls for ceremonial cleaning or sacrifice to make them acceptable in his presence, just glorious worship to the glorious one.

Illegal Worship!

This is astonishing because what David was doing was basically against the edicts of the law of Moses. Perhaps being King of Israel helped, but somehow his illegal worship service was honoured by God. God's presence blessed and didn't kill; it sanctified and didn't slay.

For thirty-three years there was non-stop worship, praise, adoration, thanksgiving, shouting, clapping, hymns, psalms, spiritual songs, prayers, prophecy, petitions and intercession. Songs sung spontaneously in that tent, birthed in the presence of God, have become enduring truth for generation after generation. God wants us to extend what went on then, here and now.

David ordered it all. He designed and built the instruments. He appointed captains and chief musicians to lead worship and train the musicians and singers for excellence, to prophesy with their hands and voices. Mentoring happened through a remarkable apprentice system. The teams took turns leading the nation in worship and imparting to others.

David released a generation to come completely into God's presence. In his tent the people were enabled to fully express their worship. They praised, they thanked, and they decreed and declared the goodness of God.

By surrendering, we give God permission to transform us from one glory to another glory and become like him. He will not do this against our will. We must commit ourselves to follow his instruction – radical obedience is the key to seeing the kingdom of heaven come here on the earth. So we destroy works of the devil, we cast out that evil spirit, we heal a sickness, we invite that hungry person round for dinner, we talk to that lonely one... and as we hear and obey, his will is done. It's that simple.

We worship to encounter God

He has promised to no longer hide his face from his people (Ezekiel 39:29). One of Hebrew words translated as presence, panim, literally means face (Exodus 33). Moses pleaded with God to not send his people out without the face of God.

The presence of God is our whole reason for being. Israel followed a fire by night and a cloud by day, and their encampment was around the cloud of God's presence. He was with them, just as he promised. And he is with us always, just as Jesus promised. Yet there is more to discover as we draw closer and closer – an ever-deeper level of intimacy.

Jesus went to the cross to win our salvation, which includes our wholeness, deliverance and the outpouring of the Holy Spirit. When the Holy Spirit comes upon us we become a different person and get to be the eyes, ears hands and arms of Jesus to everyone we meet. Like the Levites who carried the ark, we become carriers of his presence.

As we prioritise the presence, we are transformed to do extraordinary things through his power. So then the captives will be freed, the sick will be healed, the poor will be fed and the outcast will be embraced. If this happens then I believe that people will have no trouble seeking God!

4
PSALMS, HYMNS &
SPIRITUAL SONGS

The praise that God inhabits

You are holy, O you who dwell in [the holy place where] the praises of Israel [are offered]. (Psalm 22:3 AMP)

We were born to live in and from the presence of God. Everything about us is hardwired to discern his presence. In my first vision for worship all those years ago, there was a tangible sense of the weighty glory of God resting on his people.

In David's tent, God has a people after his own heart, assembled in a place where they can minister to him, and he to them. So what happens there that causes people to seek him? Let's take a look at it musically.

'Davidic worship' simply means worship in the spirit of the tabernacle of David, and Psalm 148 describes the kind of praise that went on there. The Hebrew word 'hallal' translated as praise literally means: to make a show or rave about, to glory in or boast upon, to be clamorously foolish about one's adoration of God. All creation raves about and boasts in the Lord!

I like 'playing the fool,' as one of my junior school teachers wrote in a report! Yet this wonderful psalm of glorious and heavenly praise describes how foolishly uninhibited it should be, as David exemplified. The worship in his tent was exuberant and engaged the whole person. Not just an intellectual exercise, it was alive and given to the Lord with passion.

The coming of Jesus did not signal the end of this! It changed how sins were atoned for (1 John 2:2), and gave us a clearer idea of the God we worship (John 14:9). But wholehearted music, singing and dancing in praise to God will never cease.

Instead, Jesus (Matthew 27:46) and the apostles (Acts 2:34) quoted from the Psalms. We are chosen people whose purpose is to praise God (1 Peter 2:9); we should continually offer the sacrifice of praise (Hebrews 13:15-16); and we should sing psalms, hymns and spiritual songs that are full of God's truth (Colossians 3:16). We can still worship as David did.

Psalms, hymns and spiritual songs

While imprisoned in Rome around 61-63 AD, Paul wrote a letter to the churches in Ephesus. He had invested in them through several visits over the years and although far away, wanted to instruct them on Spirit-filled living. Let's take a peek at what he wrote:

Speak to one another with psalms, hymns and spiritual songs. Sing and make music in your heart to the Lord, always giving thanks to God the Father for everything, in the name of our Lord Jesus Christ. (Ephesians 5:19-20 NIV)

One of the most important gifts of the Spirit is encouragement, daily speaking words of courage to one another. We all need to be built up, strengthened and cheered up – that's why God has put us in family!

When we are filled with the Spirit, our hearts are tuned to the frequency of heaven and we begin to flow with the song of the Father. Paul urges us to speak or sing to one another using psalms, hymns and spiritual songs, out of an attitude of thankfulness. The Spirit enables us to encourage one another with what God is saying.

So what are the three kinds of sacred song Paul says that we are to speak to one another in?

1. Psalms (Greek psalmos): A psalm is a set piece of music accompanied with voice and/or instruments. As we know there is a book in the Bible full of them. A psalm is probably what in the eighties was dubbed a 'chorus', with words, music and instructions for arrangement and what particular instruments might feature.

2. Hymns (Greek humnos) (as described in Ephesians 5): These may be a spontaneous, unrehearsed songs coming from the heart of the worshipper. It does seem to fit with the idea that we should 'sing and make music in your heart to the Lord.' As we worship we sing and play out some words and/or some music in our hearts, or portions of scripture we have been reading. This can happen extemporaneously, impromptu, with little or no preparation.

The singing of a new song (Psalm 33:3, 40:3) is where all psalms begin. In David's tent, once a scribe had recorded a hymn, it became a psalm or song.

3. Spiritual songs (Greek pneumatikos): are songs of the Lord, and the word comes from the Greek pneuma, usually meaning God's Spirit or breath. Just as God speaks through his people prophetically, he sings and plays through his people. He writes the words and the melody in our hearts and we bring it forth.

It is the river of life moving through us, the overflow of our hearts and the inspired spontaneous flow from heaven. You have to tune in and listen first before you sing out, and as with all things, exercising your gifts leads to improvement and development. This flow sometimes comes as the anointing falls and we become the vessel that God fills and pour ourselves out. At other times we can stir up the song and tune into the flow.

It's good to sit and watch others who are excellent doing what they do, study them and take notes. As we apply ourselves to improve and get prayer we receive impartation – the transference of grace gifts from others moving in that area.

With songs, vocabulary is important and we get that from our reading and study.

Make room, create space

We need to make room for all three types of song in our assemblies or gatherings: songs from the book – the ones we know; songs from the heart – the new songs that flow from us as we worship; songs from the Lord – the songs he sings through us and to us.

That is prophetic worship as it has the character of prophecy, but it's not limited to the voice, as skilled musicians can prophesy powerfully on their instruments. All three types mentioned in Ephesians 5:19 are prophetic in the sense they are, or should be, God's truth set to music.

Prophetic songs

There are several different words for praise in the Bible, perhaps the most common being the following:
- *halal*, e.g. Psalm 150, as we've seen, to foolishly celebrate with sound and colour
- *yahah*, e.g. Psalm 107, to hold out the hands
- *tehillah*, e.g. Psalm 22:3, to laud with a hymn

God can inhabit any of these, but it is interesting in scripture he is only recorded as inhabiting one of these kinds of praise – *tehillah* – the hymn.

Yet you are holy, enthroned on the praises (tehillah) of Israel. (Psalm 22:3 NRSV)

So it seems that the praise God inhabits our spontaneous praise. Perhaps this is because these songs are creative and when we're being creative we are being like the Creator. I encourage you to make room for these songs in your gatherings, as they contain something of the very presence of God we seek. He loves to live in that environment.

Elsewhere in the Bible, we get an idea of what these songs of the heart really mean to God.

They are fitting, even beautiful for us to give...

Rejoice in the Lord, O you righteous! For praise [tehillah] from the upright is beautiful! (Psalm 33:1 NKJV)

Praise the Lord! For it is good to sing praises to our God;

for it is pleasant, and praise [tehillah] is beautiful. (Psalm 147:1 NKJV)

They are the garment God gives us to wear to replace despair...

To console those who mourn in Zion, to give them beauty for ashes, the oil of joy for mourning, the garment of praise [tehillah] for the spirit of heaviness; that they may be called trees of righteousness, the planting of the Lord, that he may be glorified. (Isaiah 61:3, NKJV)

They should be heard...

Oh, bless our God, you peoples! And make the voice of his praise [tehillah] to be heard. (Psalm 66:8 NKJV)

... all day long ...

And my tongue shall speak of your righteousness, and of your praise [tehillah] all the day long. (Psalm 35:28 NKJV)

... to the ends of the earth ...

According to your name, O God, so is your praise [tehillah] to the ends of the earth; your right hand is full of righteousness. (Psalm 48:10 NKJV)

... for all generations ...

So we, your people and sheep of your pasture, will give you thanks forever; we will show forth your praise [tehillah] to all generations. (Psalm 79:13 NKJV)

... forever!

In God we boast all day long, And praise [tehillah] your name forever. Selah. (Psalm 44:8 NKJV)

(Selah means that we pause to reflect while the musicians prophetically interpret the song we've just sung.).

We can also see their purpose: *He put a new song [tehillah] in my mouth, a hymn of praise to our God. Many will see and fear the LORD and put their trust in him.* (Psalm 40:3 NIV)

Psalm 40 makes the link between worship and people seeking God and being changed. It is the presence of God that causes people to seek him, and his presence is in songs from the heart! You can compare it to prayer. Sometimes we pray things that are already written, like the Lord's

Prayer. It is good to pray the Scriptures because we know it is God's will – he wrote the words, after all. But, very often we pray spontaneously as we feel inspired to do so or out of compassion for a person or situation. As it moves us, it will surely move the heart of our heavenly Father. So if we simply add music and focus on praise, we are into tehillah.

Prayer moves into prophecy as we yield to God, hear his voice and speak it out, and spontaneous praise moves into the spiritual song as we yield to God, hear his voice and sing it out. Perhaps an example of this is David being comforted in his trouble by God singing songs of deliverance around him:

You are my hiding-place; you will protect me from trouble and surround me with songs of deliverance. (Psalm 32:7 NIV)

To explore the spontaneous song further, I would like to tell the story of what happened twelve years ago in a moment of personal revelation.

Catch the Fire

In October of 2003, with my wife Donna and a couple of friends, I made a pilgrimage to a hotspot of revival in Toronto, Canada. It is now called TACF, Catch the Fire Toronto. John and Carol Arnott were hosting an international event to mark the tenth anniversary of God pouring out his blessing in that location.

Having been mightily marked in 1994/95 by the refreshing of the Holy Spirit in the UK, we were hungry for more. We were willing to go anywhere for breakthrough, and to find the Lord of the breakthrough in person.

Walking into that building on 224 Attwell Drive, Toronto is like walking into the warm embrace of the Father.

For several years we took teams from our church to that watering hole to experience the fires of revival, the manifest presence of God, deep corporate worship, effervescent joy and powerfully inspiring teaching. We witnessed many physical healings and miracles and heard wonderful testimonies of God's amazing grace and goodness.

Most of all, we experienced the Father's blessing. As for so many others, some of the deepest healing of my heart happened one-to-One in that building and on that carpet. As I went searching for the Father and found he was searching for me, combustion happened!

On one plane journey from London to Toronto the inflight movie was Chariots of Fire, the 1981 Oscar-winning historic British drama. It tells the true story of rival athletes Harold Abrahams – an English Jew running to overcome prejudice, and Eric Liddell, a devout Scottish Christian running for the glory of God.

While watching the film I was deeply affected by the way Eric Liddell ran. So unorthodox yet so fast, this lion-hearted athlete ran with his head back, rocking from side to side as if every stride, every flexing muscle, every straining sinew was an explosion of worship! In one scene he says: 'I believe God made me for a purpose, but he also made me fast...and when I run I feel his pleasure.'

I was squashed in a crowded plane watching a little screen, with plastic headphones covered in itchy foam jammed against my ears. Yet for a moment I felt that I was on my own in a massive movie theatre watching a glorious film in Technicolor. In my heart the familiar voice of God thundered. I suddenly realised something I knew, but hadn't really known until this moment. When I sing I feel God's pleasure!

God enjoys my singing whether I'm croaky and slightly out of tune, whether I'm pitching perfectly and performing, or whether I'm with a group of passionate ones pouring out our hearts. When I sing I feel his pleasure! Even now, as I recall that moment there is a resonance in my heart, a warm vibration in my chest and I sense God smiling in me.

A family affair
As I grew up, our house was always full of music. My Dad could whistle the melody of the most complex tunes while he was cooking or painting out in the conservatory. I also

remember my parents at our Scout camps making up funny songs and leading the singing around the campfire with gusto and fun.

Music came from the various rooms in our house but we liked to bag the front room hi-fi and record player to play our latest singles. I remember my first-ever vinyl album purchased with pocket money and the wonderful record collections of my brothers and sister. I loved poring over the album sleeves and looking in detail at the amazing art. They were all colours on the palette of my imagination, long before the advent of MTV and the music video!

The soundscape of my youth inspired me to music and I remember as a 12-year-old in art class drawing a picture of myself behind the world's biggest drum set. I eventually owned that drum set...well, most of it – you can never have enough toms and cymbals in my experience!

I feel God's pleasure

Just consider what do you love to do creatively more than anything else? When do you specially feel or sense his pleasure? Is it to paint, to craft, to move, to dance, to cook, to give hospitality, to be generous with time and attention, to listen, to write, to photograph, to coach, to exercise or to work?

Fill in the blank and say it out loud: When I _____ I feel God's pleasure! Go on, admit to yourself something simple and profound that stirs your heart and makes you come alive.

Whatever you do, work at it wholeheartedly as though you were doing it for the Lord and not merely for people. (Colossians 3:23)

Whatever it is, do it unto the Lord. Then you have worshipped.

Therefore, as God's chosen people, holy and dearly loved, clothe yourselves with compassion, kindness, humility, gentleness and patience. Bear with each other and forgive one another if any of you has a grievance against someone. Forgive as the Lord forgave you. And over all these virtues put on love, which binds them all together in perfect unity. (Colossians 3:12-14 NIV)

Colossians 3 is a powerful and simple instruction for godly life, listing all the things to take off and what to wear as a child of God. In describing 'kingdom fashion,' it says put on love. Perhaps we have a tendency to take it off and leave it behind in the wardrobe! If we forget to put our love on in the morning, it shows.

Let the peace of Christ rule in your hearts, since as members of one body you were called to peace. And be thankful. Let the message of Christ dwell among you richly as you teach and admonish one another with all wisdom through psalms, hymns, and songs from the Spirit, singing to God with gratitude in your hearts. (Colossians 3:15-16, NIV)

This great passage admonishing us to reveal God's heart to each other with thankful hearts in psalms, hymns and spiritual songs, finishes with this simple instruction of worship as a way of life:

And whatever you do, whether in word or deed, do it all in the name of the Lord Jesus, giving thanks to God the Father through him. (Colossians 3:17 NIV)

Whatever you do, work at it with all your heart, as working for the Lord, not for human masters, since you know that you will receive an inheritance from the Lord as a reward. It is the Lord Christ you are serving. (Colossians 3:23-4 NIV)

Whatever you do, do it as if you are doing it for Jesus. Do it for him alone, and give it to him full of gratitude. Picture him before you as you do whatever it is you are doing and that is truly worship.

In return, we are rewarded with an inheritance. We build for his glory now and also for the future glory that others get to walk in after us. The Kingdom of Heaven is our inheritance and every expression of worship lays the bricks of that kingdom.

There are times when the enemy tries to shut my mouth and a song is far from my lips. Yet when I realise what's going on, I choose to return to releasing my heart through melody. When we pray, the secrets of our hearts overflow. It's the same when we sing spontaneously – the rushing brook of our heart flows out, hopefully sweet, clean waters!

Whether I am in my bedroom with my guitar, in my office with headphones on, in the kitchen cooking with a melody going through my head, on stage with my eyes shut unaware of anyone else, or standing in the congregation with my head back and my heart on fire, arms spread high and wide and worshipping with everything that is in me, when I sing I sense God's pleasure.

As a child I had a toy guitar and used to sing at home with my Mum. I can remember my mother's beautiful smile as I toddled around singing spontaneous made-up songs. These smudgy snapshots of childhood moments foreshadow what I have been doing most of my adult life.

Just as Jesus multiplied the little boy's offering to feed thousands, God has a wonderful way of doing amazing things with our offerings that we could perhaps never imagine. Here's a recent example.

A spiritual song

While I stood in the congregation at Bethel, Redding, a time of worship flowed into a spontaneous congregational song. It was just an outpouring of joyful noise by many singing out in their native tongues or their heavenly language. I dearly love the freedom of these precious times when there is enough volume in the room to raise my voice to sing loudly.

With all my strength I just let rip, in a way that was deep and satisfying. It became an extraordinary moment for me, as during the singing I saw a sweeping visual of myself singing in the congregation with my head back and arms held high, as if from a camera on a large boom arm. The lights in the room intensified, with swirls of colours and white lights whooshing around. Then I began to float upwards and was suspended off the ground. My body was surrounded by a spiral swirl of light, like a kind of whirlwind in slow motion... And then the same thing was happening to others, who floated up and were surrounded by bright lights and colours as they sang out and worshipped.

There was a wonderful tumult of sound and vibration being released in that place. This corporate heart-song echoed around the room for many minutes and I continued to pour out my thankfulness and joy to the Lord, catching glimpses of his majestic glory.

After a while the ebb and flow of sound quietly died down to just the soft notes on the keyboard. I could almost feel myself gently returning to the ground. A little while later when we were invited to greet and bless someone nearby, the lady in front of me turned and shared what had just happened to her during the worship...

For many years she had wanted to hear the sound of God singing over her. She knew the verse in Zephaniah 3:17 very well – 'the Lord takes delight in you and rejoices over you with singing' and had often asked God to hear that song. As I sang my song wholeheartedly to God, he took it and sang over her, telling her that my song was just for her, a personal gift to one of his special daughters! She was deeply moved and hugged me fiercely and it was so humbling that she had received a personal touch from the Father through me. I was stunned – the Lord used something I gave freely to him to draw another person into a greater intimacy with him. It was the profound manifestation of a prophetic spiritual song which I shall remember for a very long time.

Prophetic songs and music

David had a clear vision of what he wanted in his tent. He expected excellence and to help achieve that, he appointed people specifically to lead, to teach and to train in prophetic songs and in prophetic music:

Kenaniah the head Levite was in charge of the singing; that was his responsibility because he was skilful at it. (1 Chronicles 15:22 NIV)

The Hebrew word translated 'singing' here is massa, meaning prophetic burden, and the word for skilled is sakal, which implies being understanding, intelligent, wise and considerate, as well as gifted, trained and experienced. So Kenaniah was not just a great musician, but had wisdom and understanding, so he was used to train others in prophetic singing.

Prophetic music

Words are containers of thought, and music can transport those thoughts directly into our hearts.

David, together with the commanders of the army, set apart some of the sons of Asaph, Heman and Jeduthun for the ministry of prophesying, accompanied by harps, lyres and cymbals. (1 Chronicles 25:1, NIV)

So that is prophetic singing to the sound of low-strung and high-strung instruments and percussion. Hopefully we can grasp that music is prophetic almost by nature, and its sound can shift the atmosphere around us. The character of music conveys a message that bypasses the mind and brings about an emotional response.

Take the music out of movies, for example, and we probably wouldn't laugh so much at the funny bits, cry so much at the sad bits, squeeze a cushion during the tense bits and hide behind the sofa at the scary bits. Take the music out of advertising and shopping malls and we probably wouldn't buy so many things we don't actually need!

Martin Luther believed that every child should study music because it trains the spirit in worship and worship is eternal. Yet the church's reaction to contemporary music has so often been unhealthy, tossing the tattooed rock baby out with the bath water! Historically the church has subjectively defined what is good and what is evil, when it is likely to be more to do with personal taste or preference. In so doing, creative voices are silenced and certain artists are demonised.

'Why should the devil have all the good music?' was an anthem of the early seventies from singer-songwriter Larry Norman, the voice of the Jesus Movement. It became hugely popular in counter-cultural Christianity. While religious voices condemned, the creative ones kept on releasing what God had put in their hearts.

Charles Wesley was a prolific writer and some 4,400 hymns and poems are accredited to him. His prophetic songs accompanied the move of God sweeping through England in the eighteenth century. Some still regularly feature in church services such as 'Hark the Herald Angels Sing,' 'Oh for a Thousand Tongues,' 'Love Divine, All Loves Excelling,' and 'Christ the Lord is Risen Today.'

The hymns were Charles's poetry set to music, and the tunes were easy to sing. Words and music combined to teach and reinforce the key theological and spiritual convictions of Methodism. Remember, this movement was birthed in shouting, singing and clapping, groaning and crying, praying and exhorting!

Some people whinge about modern songs because they believe the traditional is more pure, yet at some point in time those hymns were new! The founder of the Salvation Army, William Booth, set heart-changing words of truth to familiar, contemporary tunes. He also wrote songs to be sung at their evangelistic campaigns, notably 'Boundless Salvation' in 1893.

Another song of that era entitled 'Just as I Am' was written by Charlotte Elliot in 1835. A young Billy Graham heard those words, set to William B. Bradbury's tune, at the point of his salvation in 1934. Graham then used that song at the altar call of every crusade he did for 40 years! It's estimated that 3.2 million people have responded to Christ through his life, ministry and message, and at every altar call the words resonate around the tents and arenas and stadiums.

Just as I am, without one plea,
But that Thy blood was shed for me,
And that Thou bidst me come to Thee,
O Lamb of God, I come!

It seems that new songs all have a key role alongside the great moves of God. 'Here is Love, Vast as the Ocean' is the sound of the Welsh Revival. This anthem still brings heaven to earth over a hundred years after it was composed, as I witnessed just a couple of years ago at a Global Awakening Kingdom Foundations conference in Cardiff.

We invited a local artist to sing with us one night and she performed the most powerful rendition of this wonderful hymn I have ever heard. She sang first in Welsh and then in English, with such passion and commitment that when we joined in it felt like the earth was trembling with the sound. The prophetic nature of that song still stirs the fires of revival in burning hearts!

A style of music in itself is not evil, an instrument in itself is not evil and anything can be redeemed before the cross. Simply put: bad people can put music to bad use, and good people can use music for good. Music and emotions are still good – as God made them, and the Creator created us to be creative! So it is right that we use our gifts, our music and our songs as God intended.

Prophetic music prepares our emotions to receive what God is saying by conveying the sense of it. So soothing music will help us receive his love, marching music will help us receive his instruction to go, and pounding music will help us engage with him in warfare.

Many of the psalms come with instructions for how they are to be played and on what instruments, to best convey the message. For example Psalm 4 is a neginoth which requires stringed instruments, Psalm 5 is a nehiloth which requires flutes, Psalm 7 is a shiggaion which requires wild, frenzied rhythms, Psalm 22 is to be sung to the tune of 'The doe of the morning,' however that goes ... though I think it's in the heavenly key of Bb!

Some psalms specify selahs, which are generally believed to be musical interludes where the singing stopped and the musicians interpreted the words. There are three in Psalm 3: the first is after verses 1-2 where David is surrounded by his enemies, so perhaps the music would convey danger. The second is after verses 3-4 where David cries out to God to rescue him, so perhaps the music would convey hope. The third is after verses 5-8 where God defeats his enemies, so that music might convey victory.

I won't try to identify and define all the musical terms used in the Bible here. But it's worth becoming familiar with scriptural directions for worship: what instrumentation is suitable for certain songs and which frequency. God ordained that words and music should work together in prophetic songs and that people should be trained in leading them.

In practice, once we have given time to spontaneous praise, someone in the assembly may sing out a prophetic song. Then the skilled musicians may respond with music that conveys the meaning, cementing the message in the hearts of those assembled, which in turn may inspire further prophetic songs. As we move with the Holy Spirit our desire should be to overflow with purpose and intensity.

Prophetic song for a city
Some time ago our church band occasionally travelled with Graham Cooke as he did his prophetic ministry across the UK and in Europe. On one occasion we were in Liverpool and Graham had a word for the city that he wanted to deliver in a new way, partly spoken and then with song.

The idea was that the people of Liverpool would continue to sing the truth of what God was saying to them in the months and years to follow. The word called forth salvation, encouraging transformation with the empowering thought that the battle is the Lord's!

There is something quite profound about turning prophecy into a song. We rarely repeat a prophetic word that has been spoken but we often sing songs week after week. A song encases truth in music and melody which is then released into the spiritual atmosphere. Remember that faith comes by hearing, and what we decree can and will take place if it comes from the Father.

Graham had divided his word into several sections, each one condensed into a verse of the song. My brother Nigel and I spent some time crafting this to interpret the message in each verse; the chorus was a decree in itself. The prayer and preparation that went into the song was a vital ingredient.

On the day, Graham spoke the first part of his word and we sung the first verse and the chorus. Then Graham delivered the next part of his word and we sung the next verse and chorus and so on. At the end of the prophecy we invited the whole conference to stand and sing in unison our song, 'Jesus Lives in the City.'

It was a special moment in the host church, and that song was sung for many years after our conference, decreeing again and again who is the Lord of Liverpool!

Here's an extract:

Verse 1
The voice of God is calling; the time for change is here.
Your Spirit falls upon all flesh releasing those who fear
To reap a mighty harvest across the city streets.
Our God will give us a victory where we place our feet
As we receive anointing make us champions for you
And in our restoration your power will break through.

Chorus
Jesus lives in the city;
His purposes will be fulfilled.
He will restore his name, his place, his kingdom
In our hearts and lives ... let the work begin.

Recently we've seen an increase of music and songs with a strong prophetic edge. In a number of videos on YouTube and recordings on the internet, the song continues as musicians and singers develop the sound, interpret the truth and improvise, taking the congregation and the listener into deeper places in worship.

There is a wonderful freedom in worship when the song is over but the overflowing heart hasn't run out of things to sing, declare or prophecy. Some houses of prayer live-stream their 24/7 output, so worship, prayer, intercession and the truth of scripture are all flying around the information superhighway.

Sing like David

The psalms of David released a promise for future generations and are still vibrantly alive today. How often has your head been lifted after reading the psalms? How many times have you been comforted or encouraged? That's because someone wrote it down when the inspired thought came. We move from despair into peace because of his living and active word resonating in our hearts. When we read it we feel like running again!

We also need to record what God is doing and saying among us so we can give him glory for it all and inspire others with the testimony or the song. We remember, we recount, and our hearts resound with praise and thanksgiving. When you value what God has done in the past, there is an invitation to release it in the present, in the here and now.

I suspect David had scribes to record events, songs and prophetic decrees in the tabernacle. 1 Chronicles 15:4 implies that some were appointed to record or remember in the tent, so many of the songs in the book of Psalms could have been written there. Decrees and declarations made in that tent have continued to be made throughout history and translated into almost every language used on the planet!

There is something about worship in the glory that positions us for something extraordinary in our lives. Ordinary people step into the atmosphere of heaven, clothed in righteousness to declare, decree and proclaim the word of the Lord!

I will proclaim the Lord's decree: He said to me, 'You are my son; today I have become your father. Ask me, and I will make the nations your inheritance, the ends of the earth your possession.' (Psalm 2:7-8 NIV)

Encounter in Brazil

There are moments in this Christian life that mark us for eternity. One such point for me was during a Global Awakening International ministry trip with Randy Clark in Uberlandia, Brazil in 2009. We had taken part in a revival service with an intense sense of the presence of God. It was like an old tent meeting as the large marquee had no proper flooring, just sawdust, pieces of cardboard and old carpet scattered here and there.

Possibly over a thousand people sat on plastic garden chairs. As Randy and the team ministered, hundreds of people were healed. There were over one hundred commitments to Jesus that night including many youth and children. During a time of 'impartation' (the transference of anointing), people were tremendously affected by the power (energia) of Holy Spirit.

Some people are quick to say, 'That's not God' and judge things that don't line up with their experience or understanding. Yet God's ways are not ours and on this evening I saw well-groomed men and fashionably dressed ladies fall to the floor and roll around on damp cardboard and sawdust! They seemed unconcerned about appearances or the fact their clothes were getting covered in mud as they encountered the Lord in a profound way. People were physically shaking, crying out, and laughing uncontrollably as they were touched by heaven. Etched into my memory was a couple of boys with arms around each other's shoulders on the 'mercy seat' of the stage platform. They were both weeping uncontrollably and the glasses of one of the young lad had steamed up with his tears. I believe a child of his age could not pretend and he had been unforgettably touched by a loving Saviour.

Afterwards we left the tent and gathered in another room for refreshments. Somehow we ended up laying hands on and praying for the leadership of the host church. Then people started praying for me and I was immediately taken to another place 'in the Spirit' as hands were laid on me. I felt an immense weight and pressure, with warmth and energy flowing through me.

Then the worship pastor Gustavo Paiva came to me and started praying in Portuguese. There was a sense of anticipation that something significant was about to happen. I vaguely heard someone translating, but was grateful that I'd set my phone recording before all this started!

He made a fist with his hand and placed it over my chest. It felt extremely hot and as though his hand went through my ribcage and grabbed my heart. At that point I fell backwards to the ground, crying out loudly. I still had the overwhelming sensation of an intense, burning hand around my heart as Gustavo leant down and finished prophesying over me. After a few more moments I heard him finish praying, stand up and walk away clapping, yet the weighty sensation on my ribcage and over my heart was still there!

I've learnt over years not to get up until the Holy Spirit has finished what he is doing, because in that kind of encounter, something is deposited in your heart that will come no other way. Willing for God to do whatever he wanted, I lay there until the waves subsided and finally the pressure in my chest lifted off.

Later, Gustavo's spiritual son Mario translated the prayer for me, and then another sign that makes me wonder happened. As he was listening to the recording on my phone, flakes of gold appeared all over his hands!

This is the translated prayer from Pastor Gustavo:

Father God, give him a new anointing. Take his sound to a new level in the spiritual realm. God has been giving us in Brazil, worship that will touch the world. As you gave me a heart of David in Israel, please release an angel – the same angel to come and touch his change and change his heart.

This was the point when my chest was invaded angelically and I fell to the ground shouting!

The sound of your lips will change. The sound of your hands will change from today because your heart has been changed. Today I impart over your life what God put over me: the sound of heaven! The sound of heaven! The sound of heaven! It will not be from the earth, it will be from heaven, because your heart is different ... more, more, more!

(He stood and walked off clapping). Sometime later, as I was still receiving on the floor, he came back and added:

Forget the method, forget the formulas, because God wants to give you a new sound...

Something really did change in me when I ministered in worship after that. A tangible depth was added to what I already carried. I remind myself from time to time what God said through a faithful servant and what I experienced; the physical manifestations seem to help to cement the truth in my heart. Sometimes words can be missed, lost or forgotten – that's why I use a recorder. But an encounter with God can change you, 'from one degree of glory to another.'

I share this not to sound proud but because I would love others to have a similar experience for themselves. Maybe it will sound tame to some of you because of your many visits to heaven! But for others, it could be a new concept of how God can meet with each one of us personally. I have found this is the way he likes it, up close and personal.

I cherish my encounters with God because each one has touched and marked me in some way. Some have brought revelation, some have brought vision of his nature and truth, some have brought healing and inner healing, and some have activated gifts in me. Some are so deep that they are still being gradually processed on my journey with him.

Just as Jacob walked with a limp forever from a wrestling match for a blessing, God marked my heart with a sound of heaven. He did something to me that I have taken hold of intentionally. I thank God for his loving kindness and the countless way he speaks, and I also honour his living, active word over my life.

Now it doesn't take much to flow with the Spirit and engage my heart in outpouring. When I pick up a guitar and sing, sometimes 'psalms,' sometimes spontaneous 'hymns' and at other times, flowing with the rivers of living water coming from my innermost being, I release 'spiritual songs' for individuals or groups or a city or region, prophesying with my voice or with a drum or guitar.

I believe it's my primary calling on earth to lead people into his presence. On this wonderful journey, a few years ago I was taken to another level through impartation and a touch from God.

Sound of heaven

As worshippers we are here to release heaven on earth with a magnificent sound that vibrates like the Holy Spirit hovering over the waters of creation. It's a sound that pulses with the steady heartbeat of heaven and draws people into encounter with a loving Father. This kind of worship may one day attract the glory of the Lord so powerfully that the service is interrupted by the arrival of the King!

5
INVITATION TO ENCOUNTER

A watering hole encounter

Travel with me if you will through the heat and the dust, to a little town called Sychar, in Samaria. At high noon one day, Jesus was weary from his journey back to Galilee from Judea. He decided to rest a while by Jacob's well and sent his lads off to fetch some groceries, knowing that he had a divine appointment with a heart searching for love.

A woman from Samaria came to draw water. Jesus said to her, 'Give me a drink' (for his disciples had gone away into the city to buy food.) The Samaritan woman said to him, 'How is it that you, a Jew, ask for a drink from me, a woman of Samaria?' (for Jews have no dealings with Samaritans). Jesus answered her, 'If you knew the gift of God, and who it is that is saying to you, "Give me a drink," you would have asked him, and he would have given you living water.'

The woman said to him, 'Sir, you have nothing to draw water with, and the well is deep. Where do you get that living water? Are you greater than our father Jacob? He gave us the well and drank from it himself, as did his sons and his livestock.' Jesus said to her, 'Everyone who drinks of this water will be thirsty again, but whoever drinks of the water that I will give him will never be thirsty again. The water that I will give him will become in him a spring of water welling up to eternal life.' (John 4:7-14 CEV)

Once again we get a glimpse of the importance of legacy. Jacob dug that well which signified wealth for his herds and his family. Yet many years on, this life-giving well became a place where eternally living waters flowed. That watering hole was destined to be a place for revival, as many from the village came into a real relationship with Jesus...

In the conversation, Jesus reveals his Father's desire for all his children and the simple and profound meaning of worship.

The woman said to him, 'Sir, give me this water, so that I will not be thirsty or have to come here to draw water.' Jesus said to her, "Go, call your husband, and come here.' The woman answered him, 'I have no husband.' Jesus said to her, 'You are right in saying, "I have no husband"; for you have had five husbands, and the one you now have is not your husband. What you have said is true.' The woman said to him, 'Sir, I perceive that you are a prophet. Our fathers worshiped on this mountain, but you say that in Jerusalem is the place where people ought to worship.'

Jesus said to her, 'Woman, believe me, the hour is coming when neither on this mountain nor in Jerusalem will you worship the Father. You worship what you do not know; we worship what we know, for salvation is from the Jews. But the hour is coming, and is now here, when the true worshipers will worship the Father in spirit and truth, for the Father is seeking such people to worship him. God is spirit, and those who worship him must worship in spirit and truth.' The woman said to him, 'I know that Messiah is coming (he who is called Christ). When he comes, he will tell us all things.' Jesus said to her, 'I who speak to you am he.'

Just then his disciples came back. They marvelled that he was talking with a woman, but no one said, 'What do you seek?' or, 'Why are you talking with her?' So the woman left her water jar and went away into town and said to the people, 'Come, see a man who told me all that I ever did. Can this be the Christ?' They went out of the town and were coming to him. (John 4:15-30 CEV)

So what rocked the world of the Samaritan woman so completely? She was at first focused on her own life and her own needs: 'Sir, give me this water, so that I will not be thirsty or have to come here to draw water.' Yet as she spoke to Jesus her heart was being awakened.

Jesus came to reveal the Father on the earth and this came shining through. Knowing everything about her private history, he deliberately stepped across a cultural divide of stigma, religion and legalism. He demonstrated the Father's love, not just to any daughter, but one of his favourites. I think Jesus sent his boys away so he could have a one-to-one without any interruptions from his well-meaning companions.

Her questions to him came from an obligation to worship by law, yet her lifestyle demonstrated a different drive. Inside she was looking for a real and meaningful love and a deeper relationship with God. Jesus continued with his revelations...

'The time is coming when you will worship [Daddy, Papa, Abba] in spirit and in truth.'

'The time is coming when you will proskuneo.' This is translated as worship, yet literally means to move towards and kiss. It's intimate and meaningful. The Father's arms are described as everlasting (Deuteronomy 33:27) because he wants to give each and every one of us a really big hug! He offers us a place of safety and a place to dwell, and he enjoys our loving kisses.

When my daughter was a toddler and still called me Daddy, I loved it when she crawled onto my lap and put her tiny arms around my neck and kissed me. That is the worship that the Father seeks. Come and kiss him, and be kissed in return.

As the Samaritan woman was talking with Jesus, their conversation was all about the 'how', 'where', 'when' and 'why' of worship. Yet the result was a revelation of the Father's love for one broken daughter. She was married five times and was currently living with another man. In her relationships with men, she was searching for what can only be discovered in a pure relationship with Papa, with Daddy.

Jesus carried the Heavenly Father's perfect love with him and leaked it into the heart of this searching one, so her desire was changed from man to God, from the created to the Creator. Her longing for love was finally realigned. Not only was her life was changed irrevocably, but that woman became an evangelist sharing the message of Jesus to her whole village.

Jesus didn't tell her to go onto the mission field; the revelation had taken hold of her heart. Forgetting why she had come to the well in the first place, she ran back into her village to tell everybody about Jesus and release what she had just received. Jesus may never have received his cup of water! Once she had received the Father's love she naturally had to give it away.

Many believed and were saved, first by what she said, and then through their own encounter with the Messiah.

Many Samaritans from that town believed in him because of the woman's testimony, 'He told me all that I ever did.' So when the Samaritans came to him, they asked him to stay with them, and he stayed there two days. And many more believed because of his word. They said to the woman, 'It is no longer because of what you said that we believe, for we have heard for ourselves, and we know that this is indeed the Saviour of the world.' (John 4:39-42 CEV)

Long after it was dug, Jacob's well remained a life-giving place to those who visited it and those who dwelt nearby.

Watering holes

'Watering holes' and places of refreshing provide a safe place for people to come to the source of living water. Part of restoring David's tabernacle must be establishing such places of renewal and revival. Often in recent years, there have been 'outpourings' where the Holy Spirit is visibly moving in a city or church. Yet there is a call to sustain kingdom-focussed environments where this kind of outpouring isn't transitory but ongoing.

God's people can deliberately live in a way that overflows with transforming love: a life of encounter. Once we are filled with the Father's love and healed of our orphan-hearted tendencies, we will naturally flow into devotion and worship in spirit and in truth.

One to one

It's all about encounter – personal and corporate; inward, upward and outward. We make an inward journey of the heart, being known by Father, Son and Holy Spirit. The essential aspect of the Christian life is personal intimacy with God. No one else can have your relationship with God for you: he wants to know you and wants you to know him.

Moses prayed 'let me know your ways that I may know you.' As we find out more about his nature we get to learn more about him, and that is what transforms us from the inside out. Jesus came to bring grace and truth, grace for what we have done and truth about who we are. When we know the truth we are set free to soar.

Then we have corporate encounter through relationships in the church that encourage, strengthen and comfort. We share our personal encounters in a way that brings the presence to each other. While speaking words of hope and courage we release each other to go out and impact our sphere of influence on a daily basis.

Whatever we receive we need to share, just as the Samaritan woman did. Freely you have received, so freely give it away! We give away the revelation we have received in our encounters with him.

Jesus, me and a cup of tea

On one of my trips to Brazil I had an extraordinary experience. The power of God came on me in such a way I could not stand, as if fire and electricity were coursing through my body. It was intense, yet also fun, in a strange kind of way. While it was happening I was overwhelmed by joy, and laughter –

it was just bubbling up inside of me and pouring out! This would have been fine if I had been sitting at the back of the church unobserved, but I wasn't. I was standing on a large stage in full view of hundreds, if not thousands of people! A video camera in my hand, I had been documenting Randy Clark ministering during a healing service; the people being spontaneously healed and their testimonies afterwards.

A friend of mine, pastor Ed Rocha was translating for Randy at the time. We were about 15 meters apart, yet simultaneously knocked to the ground under the power of Holy Spirit as if a team of rugby-playing angels had tackled both of us. Strangely, I didn't break the expensive camera I was holding!

I vaguely heard Randy calling for a replacement interpreter but wasn't at all bothered because of the deep connection I was having with Papa. It's not the first time something like this has happened to me, yet part of my brain always 'tilts' a bit when it does. My rational side is inclined to sort myself out, dust myself off and walk quietly to a back room, while my passionate heart is vibrantly alive as I realise this is a sovereign meeting with Almighty God.

At such moments I choose to let God do what he wants to do, however foolish I may look. I have found that I am always changed on the inside in some meaningful way, whatever it looks to the casual observer. And frankly there are times when I have to choose to go lower.

Anyway, on this extraordinary occasion, I lay on the stage feeling waves of love and joy and the pulsing power of God in my body. After some time, I realised that Ed, who was previously lying some distance away, was somehow right there next to me! This made us both laugh uncontrollably all the more. I managed in my weakened state to reach over and pray and prophesy over Ed despite still seeming stuck to the floor.

Later that night, Ed told me of a vision he saw while we were on the stage together:

He saw me standing on hard ground like old grey industrial concrete which was everywhere. I was swinging a sledgehammer trying to smash the ground, banging away with all my force. But the hammer would just bounce off, barely leaving a mark.

Then Ed saw Jesus come along smiling and laughing, drinking a cup of tea. I think I was a little put out that Jesus was laughing at my efforts, but he was just full of joy. Jesus called to me to come over, so I immediately dropped the sledgehammer and went to him. He passed me a cup of tea and I caught the twinkle in his eyes. He started laughing again and I began to laugh with him.

Then suddenly, the hard ground beneath my feet began to crack until it broke apart. All around the cracks widened and the hard ground crumbled to dust and became a rich, dark earth. Then plants and grass began to sprout and grow in fluid motion all around.

All the while Jesus and I carried on laughing and sipping our tea together. In what seems no time at to Ed in his vision, all the landscape was transformed into a beautiful flowering meadow with fruit trees, shrubs and bushes.

That vision spoke deep into a part of my heart which was still striving. Later I took a moment to repent and let go of trying to make things happen with my own effort. Instead, I was able to relax and enjoy the company of my laughing Saviour without the need to prove myself, because I had a revelation of his approval over my life.

I've learned to listen very closely to what God says during these encounters, however odd or strange they seem. He really does know better than I do, and when he speaks it brings encouragement. God may want to correct my course or prune something, but always brings words of strength and life that lead to fruitfulness and growth.

Jesus is the one who comes running when we get into a scrape. He picks us up, dusts us off and even laughs until all the stress and worry slip away. We too can laugh as we see his victory manifesting in our lives. He wants the victory even more than we do, and I've found that he's very intentional about it.

What he seeks

Yet a time is coming and has now come when the true worshippers will worship the Father in the Spirit and in truth, for they are the kind of worshippers the Father seeks. (John 4:24 NIV)

Jesus says the Father is looking for one thing: not worship but worshippers. God is not an egotist in need of my affirmation. He is a Father looking for his children and he wants them to be restored to him. He is a father searching for orphans and the orphan-hearted, to place them back into family. When we personally receive his unconditional love, it challenges and changes us.

Our 'Ark of Agreement' is a resounding yes to the Father. Give thanks to the Lord because his love endures forever. Let's worship him, let's thank him, and let's praise him!

God wants the best for me!

There's a thought. Depending on your background, personality type, life experiences, feelings of unworthiness and so on, you may find it difficult to believe... But go on, why don't you say that out loud? 'God wants the best for me!'

God loves each and every one of us, and I know that the best for me is to be like Jesus. The best for you is to be just like him too. That means peaceful yet with great authority, full of joy yet acquainted with grief, strong and very gentle, wise, obedient, loving, and sacrificial. There are many more amazing attributes of our Saviour that he wants to be hallmarks in our lives.

It involves dying so that we may live, losing ourselves to find ourselves, being pruned to become fruitful, becoming the least so that we may become great, becoming humble so that we may be lifted up, becoming obedient to be entrusted with influence, and so on. The character, wisdom and power we seek are the flip side of the same lifestyle that formed it in Jesus himself.

In transforming encounters, our minds get renewed and we change the way we think. And as we mine the golden words of hope he places deep in our hearts, we continue this wonderful adventure.

The Samaritan woman's encounter with Jesus took her from a life searching for love, to one where she pointed people to love. Her testimony became a sign for others to follow. I believe the Lord is searching the earth for those that truly love him. He is also *'the rewarder of those that diligently seek him'* (Hebrews 11:6 NKJV).

In the King James translation the word diligently is used, and in other translations there are words like 'earnestly.' We are not religiously striving to find God who has already made himself available and visible. Yet there is something about seeking and finding, drawing near and being intentional in our personal relationship with our Father.

Jesus speaks of those the Father seeks, who worship in Spirit and in truth. He wants passionate worshippers who are pursuing excellence. We are neither to be lukewarm and comfortable with mediocrity, nor striving in perfectionism.

For me, it's about intentionality. The writer of Hebrews encourages us to be faithful and diligent in seeking the Lord as he reward us with new levels of revelation and understanding. As we seek him in scripture, speak and listen to him in prayer, and sing our worship, we are drawn near to the one who said he will hide his face from us no longer.

'Due diligence' means an investigation or a comprehensive appraisal. It is good to seek out deeper truth, to be diligent in your search, to be hungry in your quest, relentless in your pilgrimage and passionate in your pursuit of all that God is.

On a Bethlehem hillside the shepherds who witnessed the awesome proclamation of the angelic host did not return to their campfires; they went into Bethlehem and sought out Jesus. The wise men weren't content to gaze at a cosmic phenomenon; they got on their camels and followed the star sign to Jesus.

Here are a few other examples of people passionate about encountering Jesus. John and Andrew wanted his home address (John 1:39); the Greeks gate-crashed a party and demanded of the host 'please, we want to see Jesus!' (John 12:20), Matthew invited Jesus into his house (Matthew 9:10), and Zacchaeus climbed a tree for a glimpse of him in the crowd (Luke 19).

Bartimaeus was not put off by those who would discourage him, but shouted all the louder for Jesus (Mark 10:46-52). His passion stopped Jesus in his tracks; ours can do the same. What normally follows is some kind of invitation: 'Come up here!'

Praise and thanksgiving lead us through the gates into his courts, but wholehearted worship leads us to the altar and to encounter. It is there that God reveals himself; he will not share his heart in a hurry. He wants us to enter the garden of his presence, enjoy the blooms and the fragrance, marvel at the beauty and linger a little longer, until the beating of his heart changes the tempo of our lives.

We need to risk whatever it takes to see Jesus, the Christ, the anointed one! God rewards those who seek him. Not those who seek doctrine or religion, systems and creeds, or any lesser passions. God rewards those who seek him out. The reward goes to those who settle for nothing less than Jesus himself.

Exchange through encounter

Divine exchange happens through encounter; as we draw near to him, he draws near to us. But God also wants to go deeper in us.

And we all, with unveiled face, beholding the glory of the Lord, are being transformed into the same image from one degree of glory to another. For this comes from the Lord who is the Spirit. (2 Corinthians 3:18 ESV)

We all radiate the Lord's glory. His light shining in our hearts reveals the knowledge of that glory in the earth, the face of Jesus himself (2 Corinthians 4:6). That letter written on human hearts, not tablets of stone, is there to be read by everyone. Our journey, our profession of faith, and our persistence through suffering all reveal his glorious grace in our lives and tell the world of a good, good Father.

We become like that which we behold. When we worship him, more happens than just words being said or sung, or tunes being played. There is a paradigm shift possible that brings about transformation.

Let's be clear. We worship God because he is God and therefore worthy of it. It involves passion, commitment and sacrifice to align our hearts, minds and wills with him. We must ascribe ultimate worth to him as opposed to anyone or anything else.

It's for his benefit, not ours. Yet scandalously, worship is about the best thing we can do for ourselves because of what God graciously does to us when we worship him. It does us good to contemplate him and to re-calibrate our value system accordingly.

As we enter into worship together, we are brought into a local, corporate experience of God's omnipresence (Psalm 100:2, 2 Chronicles 3:11-14). Besides giving us a tangible understanding of our eternal life, it is also a potent form of evangelism. In the presence, philosophical questions about the existence of God become obsolete!

And our hearts are lifted up above the things we struggle with circumstantially, relationally, spiritually, and physically (Psalm 27:4-6). When we see these things from his eternal perspective (Colossians 3:1-4) they take on more manageable proportions. This means that worship is healing for those among us who are struggling. God comes, willing and able to minister to the needy.

The new covenant is built on a changed inner reality – Christ in us (Colossians 1:27). Biblicists and strivers take note:

neither information nor willpower will transform us, only an encounter with reality. It's not what we believe, or try to believe, that transforms us, but what we experience as real.

2 Corinthians 3:7-4:6 describes how when we became believers, the veil that prevented us contemplating the glory of God in the face of Christ was removed. Our imaginations are not just the vehicle for make-believe; they are the venue for genuine encounter. As we contemplate his beauty, love, joy and peace, not only are we spiritually enabled to see it ever more clearly but, miraculously, we begin to take on those qualities ourselves.

Finally, worship is an act of spiritual warfare. Our enemies are mostly not of this world (Ephesians 6:12) and worship holds them at bay (Psalm 8:2). The best way to triumph is to get our minds off of the enemy and on to the splendour of God's holiness and his ever-enduring love (2 Chronicles 20:20-23). No darkness can remain in the presence of the light of the world. And God comes to deliver the oppressed as we worship him.

No Guilt And Shame

Jesus felt no guilt and he wants to eradicate yours. That's part of the reason he went to the cross, so we can live guilt-free. He was not ashamed of his life and he wants you to be totally free from shame. Authenticity, vulnerability and positive relationships will all help break shame off your life.
Run into his presence, and flee from shame!

After King David came to his senses about his appalling sins following his adultery with Bathsheba, the cry of his heart was: *'Do not cast me from your presence or take your Holy Spirit from me'* (Psalm 51:11 NIV).

Our instinct when we fall short or mess things up is often to run away from God's presence when the very thing we need to do is to run to it! Our shame is the chain that holds us back from his promise. But God gives courage for all the challenges we face.

Shame will tell you who you are not, and it will keep you from the Voice that will tell you who you are. (Paul Manwaring)

Shame has been paid for in full by Jesus, so we need to realise that it is permanently dealt with. He took all the punishment so we can allow our hearts to be touched by his perfect grace. All the shame is washed away in the embrace of heaven's everlasting arms. When we become free from shame we inherit a double portion!

Instead of your shame you will have a double portion, and instead of humiliation they will shout for joy over their portion. Therefore they will possess a double portion in their land, everlasting joy will be theirs. (Isaiah 61:7, NASB)

Part of the prophetic promise of encounter is a double portion and overflowing joy. Enjoy it! The kingdom of God is righteousness, peace and joy in the Holy Spirit (Romans 14:17) so it's one third of the kingdom!

Jesus had no fear of death. God wants every one of us to be fearless, free from fear, with perfect love filling our heart. Let that perfect love encounter you.

Jesus demonstrated power through kindness and mercy and he wants you to have the same measure of love. You will not see the power of Jesus without first seeing his compassion. He went about doing good and healing all oppressed by the devil, because the Lord was with him (Acts 10:38).

Father God wants the best for you and the best for you is to be just like his son. Because we have all been adopted into the family, we carry the family name and have the family authority.

To quote Max Lucado:

God loves you just the way you are but he refuses to leave you that way because he wants you to be just like Jesus.

Divine exchange

In a divine exchange, the fullness of the kingdom of heaven comes and takes away something of a lesser value, replacing it with something glorious. This can be a renewed thought life, a healed body, or deliverance from a spirit of heaviness or depression. It can all happen in encounter.

Take a moment to consider a burden you may be carrying. Is it yours or is it God's? The Lord's burdens are easy. If you're not peaceful, if you are stressed, if you're carrying guilt or shame, or if the image you have of yourself doesn't match the way God sees you, then wait on him for an encounter that will transform you.

To live the worshipper's way of life, you need to travel light and full of love. The water from your innermost being needs to flow free and pure. Your thought life needs to be renewed, and the heaviness on your shoulders can be laid at the feet of Jesus. Then leave it there – don't try to pick it up again!

It's time to let go of shame and guilt so our true identity can be revealed. It's time to walk in the kind of freedom we were destined for as God's children – all creation is waiting in longing anticipation. Believe who God says you are! I encourage you to take a moment to wait on Him, turn your attention and affection to Him and invite Him to come and encounter you.

6

A WORSHIPPER'S WAY OF LIFE

A chosen people

The Father is seeking worshippers not worship – those who worship in spirit and truth. That means it's got to be authentic as God reads hearts not lips. Just going through the motions on any given Sunday is not the kind of offering he desires. He loves the overflowing expression of hearts on fire.

Even before a word is on my tongue, behold, O Lord, you know it altogether. (Psalm 139:4, NASB)

If we pontificate, position ourselves and pretend, we miss out on the real life that God wants for us. We are not here to play church. We are here to have a love encounter that transforms us, so we can bring that same transforming love to a broken world.

God's intent is to have an intimate relationship with us. When we hide our wounded hearts we avoid intimacy, which is the key to hearing his voice. Jesus said, *'My sheep hear my voice'* (John 10:27). We all, like sheep, go astray, but the Shepherd is calling us by name back into the fold.

He has called and chosen us for his purpose:

Coming to him as to a living stone, rejected indeed by men, but chosen by God and precious, you also, as living stones, are being built up a spiritual house, a holy priesthood, to offer up spiritual sacrifices acceptable to God through Jesus Christ. (1 Peter 2:4-5 NKJV)

The great temple Jesus (John 2:19) rejected by men but honoured by God, calls us to be living stones in his holy house. We have been made a royal priesthood so we can offer a sacrifice of worship that God finds acceptable.

The Hebrew verb yada means 'to know.' It is an intimate kind of knowing. We may say that we 'know' someone but simply mean we are aware of their existence, have information about them, or are their Facebook friend! However, in Hebrew thought, one can only 'know' someone if they have a close personal relationship.

Also, yada is the verb used for knowing someone sexually. Without applying it inappropriately, let's not dilute the depth of relational intimacy God is looking for with us. There comes a time between a bridegroom and his bride when the church service is over and the place for encounter is somewhere much more intimate.

Scary, isn't it? We get to be known by and to know the Creator of all things. In him we have our being and the fullness of who we are is found in him. From the beginning of time he has wanted a people to call his own.

The divine purpose

But you are a chosen generation, a royal priesthood, a holy nation, his own special people, that you may proclaim the praises of him who called you out of darkness into his marvellous light. (1 Peter 2:9 NKJV)

From the beginning God unveiled his divine purpose to have a creative community, overflowing with honour, praise, wisdom and revelation. As we pursue the most excellent way in all things we will show forth the glory God has placed on our lives.

We were purposed in the heart of God to be worshippers. When God spoke, his desire became manifest and it is still becoming manifest.

If you are not a worshipper of God you may wonder why you never come into the fullness of your calling or your reason for being on this earth. Seek God and realise He is searching for you, then wait for the fire to start.

The worship that God despises: religion on the side

During the New Year Festival in 764 BC at the sanctuary at Bethel in the northern kingdom of Israel, a group of politically secure, commercially thriving and spiritually smug Israelites gathered. Into this assembly arrived an unwelcome speaker – Amos. The message of this shepherd from the southern kingdom of Judah was unwelcome: judgement on the nations. They nearly threw him out before he could finish what God had brought him there to say.

Amos unleashed his broadside of condemnation for Israel. Their wealth was gained at the expense of the poor (Amos 2:6-8) and the righteous (5:7, 9-10), as the result of dishonest trading (8:5), bribery in court (5:12) and general withholding of justice. They were guilty of sexual immorality (2:6) and idolatry (5:26). Not only had they forgotten what God did for them in the past, to save them (2:9-10) and lead them to repentance (4:6-11), they continued to silence God's prophets in the present (2:12). Despite all this they still took great pride in their religious observance (4:4-5)! But their reward would be conquest, occupation, exile and death (3:11-15, 9:1-4).

No doubt this part of his message was not very warmly received and Amaziah, the chief priest, threw him out (7:12-13). His divine task completed, Amos returned to the obscurity he came from. In 722 BC the Assyrians invaded Israel.

Religion without righteousness

Why should I mention this, just after revelling in being a holy nation? It is because this was the context in which Amos foretold the restoration of the tabernacle of David.

'In that day I will restore David's fallen tent. I will repair its broken places, restore its ruins, and build it as it used to be, so that they may possess the remnant of Edom and all the

nations that bear my name,' declares the LORD, who will do these things. (Amos 9:11-12 NIV)

We need to know that God will not endure the religious activity of a people who are not committed to him or his cause. He wants a people that love what he loves and hate what he hates. Jesus showed this as he got angry with people who abused the poor, rejected children and misused his house.

'I hate, I despise your religious feasts; I cannot stand your assemblies. Even though you bring me burnt offerings and grain offerings, I will not accept them. Though you bring choice fellowship offerings, I will have no regard for them. Away with the noise of your songs! I will not listen to the music of your harps. But let justice roll on like a river, righteousness like a never-failing stream!' (Amos 5:21-24 NIV)

'You strum away on your harps like David and improvise on musical instruments. You drink wine by the bowlful and use the finest lotions, but you do not grieve over the ruin of Joseph. Therefore you will be among the first to go into exile; your feasting and lounging will end.' (Amos 6:5-7 NIV)

Ouch! God was not happy with his people.

Imagine if some guy smelling of sheep walked into your conference and wandered around with his fingers in his ears saying, 'I won't listen to you...what you do offends me, says the Lord!' We might ask security to escort him to the exit. But, that is what Amos did as he delivered truth like a knife to the heart of the nation. The hard-hearted didn't listen and it happened as was decreed.

Pride is an obstacle

God will not restore his presence to a proud and unholy people. He actually says he will oppose the proud and put obstacles in their path, but gives grace to the humble (Proverbs 3:34; James 4:6; 1 Peter 5:5).

To be holy means to be 'set apart for sacred use.' In other words, we must leave behind worldly things and our personal agendas and be cleaned up, filled up and placed at God's disposal. This is a challenge to all of us, but especially to those who aspire to minister to the Lord and to lead others in doing so. If we want to see God restore David's tent in our time, we must pursue holiness.

It would be great to move out of darkness and into glorious light in one fell swoop! The reality, though, is that sanctification involves both crisis and process. It's wonderful to open prison doors but enabling a former prisoner to live well in freedom involves a long process of reorientation.

Hope is often called the seedbed of faith. But hope is watered by character, which is produced by endurance (Romans 5:3-4; James 1:2-4). It took Jesus three years to make twelve disciples via a 24/7 relational, hands-on, itinerant training course. He used journey, process and mentoring: something we see happening too rarely.

I cannot impart character to someone however gifted they may be. I can prophesy, call out someone's purpose in life, and speak boldly into their destiny, yet I cannot ensure they will co-operate with God to see it fulfilled. All these things have to be worked out over time, through lifestyle and good choices. If Jesus, sinless though he was, needed a process of growth before God and people (Luke 2:52) then we can be sure we need one too.

A holy life

Some of us are afraid of the biblical call to holiness, because we feel that we can never get there. But holiness is not an unreachable star. God has a way to make us holy and it's not by human effort.

'Consecrate yourselves, therefore, and be holy, for I am the Lord your God. Keep my statutes and do them; I am the Lord who sanctifies you.' (Leviticus 20:7-8 ESV)

God is the one who sanctifies. He lights the fire on the altar, while it's the job of the priests to keep the fire burning. So we consecrate ourselves by honouring and pursuing the presence. Let us also be a glad and thankful people, reaching for gratitude in every circumstance.

Max Lucado's words have resonated in my heart since I first read them many years ago: 'Worship is the "thank you" that refuses to be silenced.' Thank you is worship. It is the heart response of the saved to the Saviour, the healed to the Healer, the delivered to the Deliverer.

Yes, there is a call on our lives to holiness, but we don't become holy to worship, we worship to become holy. Worship changes atmospheres around us and inside of us. Papa God knows that we will become like whatever we behold, or whatever we worship. So he calls us to be devoted worshippers.

Set apart for a holy purpose

Isaiah 42:8 says God will not share his glory with another... but as his chosen people we are not 'another'! He wants to share his glory with us because we are seated with him in heavenly places. Therefore we position ourselves not to get to heaven, but to bring heaven to earth. We are not working for love; we are flowing from a position of love.

So being holy is being set apart from the world and set apart for the purposes of God. In the temple the articles used in worship were anointed with holy oil (Exodus 30:22-29). When we come into a covenant relationship with God and are baptised with Holy Spirit, we are also sanctified and set apart for this holy purpose to worship.

The worship that God desires

We tend to use the word 'worship' to mean what we do in church on a Sunday, especially the bit with the singing. Now, praise, confession, thanksgiving and prayer are all vital. They all went on in David's tent and should go on now, wholeheartedly, to the glory of God. They may be inspired by, or lead us to, worship, but we should know the difference between them and true worship.

Take music. We know that God is a singer (Zephaniah 3:17, Hebrews 2:12) and because he made us in his image it is natural for us to be moved by music. The biggest book in the Bible, the Psalms, is a songbook, and some of those songs were written in the tabernacle of David so we can expect an outpouring of 'psalms, hymns and spiritual songs' in its restoration. But, while music is a key vehicle for worship it is not 'worship' as the Bible defines it.

So what is worship? God wants true worship, not just a religious activity. However, there is no equivalent for our English word 'worship' in either Greek or Hebrew. So let's look at some of the biblical vocabulary to understand this better.

David Peterson's book *Engaging With God* is a widely respected biblical theology of worship and he says that from the main word groups used in the Greek translation of the Hebrew scriptures, Old Testament worship can be summarised as: to honour (proskuneo), to serve (latreia, leiturgia) and reverently fear (phobos) God.

Under the New Covenant these words are even more full of meaning. For example, Paul uses latreia to convey our total abandonment to God's will.

Therefore, I urge you, brothers, in view of God's mercy, to offer your bodies as living sacrifices, holy and pleasing to God, this is your spiritual act of worship. (Romans 12:1 NIV)

In other words, worship is a way of life, offering our whole selves to God for his pleasure and purpose. Whatever we do when offered unto the Lord attracts his presence. So if worship means setting ourselves apart for God's use, and holiness is being set apart for God's use, then it seems worship is the way and the means to make us holy.

Proskuneo literally means prostration in homage, and moving towards to kiss, but it is also the word John uses to convey our total response to the revelation of God in Jesus.

'Yet a time is coming and has now come when the true worshipers will worship the Father in spirit and truth, for they are the kind of worshipers the Father seeks. God is spirit, and

his worshipers must worship in spirit and in truth.' (John 4:23-24 NIV)

Worship is a spiritual activity. Our spirit is the part of us that is capable of being in touch with God and under his influence. This is how our relationship with God works: his Holy Spirit connects with our spirit. For example:

The Spirit himself testifies with our spirit that we are God's children. (Romans 8:16 NIV)

So, to worship in spirit is to lovingly direct our spiritual activity towards God. This means to surrender all that makes us 'us': our minds, our emotions, our sense of right and wrong and our will to act, to the Lord. Our mandate is to do as he would do, so his will is done on earth as it is in heaven.

To truly offer ourselves to God as living sacrifices, we have to grasp the truth about him – infinite, sovereign, everlasting, loving and holy – and the truth about ourselves – dignified, loved, blessed but fallen and in need of grace.

We also need to know the truth about our relationship – he the creator and we the created, he the Lord and we the subjects, he the master and we the apprentices, he the Father and we the children, he the lover and we the beloved. We will show the world who he is by worshipping and allowing him to bless us. When we live blessed lives we demonstrate that God is good and that we are all children of a good Dad!

So we adopt a position of loving servanthood towards God – drawing near, focusing our attention on him and placing ourselves at his disposal. We see all these things in the following passage:

Then the eleven disciples went to Galilee, to the mountain where Jesus had told them to go. When they saw him, they worshiped him; but some doubted. Then Jesus came to them and said, 'All authority in heaven and on earth has been given to me. Therefore go and make disciples of all nations, baptising them in the name of the Father and of the Son and of the Holy Spirit, and teaching them to obey everything I have commanded you. And surely I am with you always, to the very end of the age.' (Matthew 28:16-20 NIV)

When they realised who he really was, they worshipped Jesus. Even in their doubts, the Spirit-filled words of Jesus brought life and confidence to his followers. He instructed them to 'Go' under his authority and reassured them that he would be with them always.

Perfect love drives out all fear (1 John 4:18), and most New Testament uses of phobos in relation to God refer to unbelievers, but some do refer to believers (e.g. Acts 9:31; 2 Corinthians 7:1; and Philippians 2:12). This means that we must still allow for the reverent fear of God. He is both our Daddy and dangerous; both trustworthy and terrifying; both comforting and consuming.

So as we 'think about such things' (Philippians 4:8), we are drawn to worship. We understand that in the grand scheme of eternity all is well (Romans 8:28-39) and that what we have been given is far greater than what we can give or any trouble we are experiencing (2 Corinthians 4:16-18). His faithfulness is great and he is with us and for us! So true worship is a key to breakthrough.

As some people have realised that true worship is a way of life, not a religious activity, they have felt disenchanted with church meetings: 'There are sick to be healed, poor to be fed, children that need families, young people to support, and disciples to be made. Why do we need church?'

God wants devotion to him so that his kingdom is established by his family on earth as it is in heaven. We are here to bring reformation. But it's only transformed people who transform the world, so each one of us needs encounters with God. When we are intimately linked to the God who knows no impossibility, we can go and conquer the seemingly impossible!

However we can't abandon church, which is what the restoration of the tabernacle of David is all about. We need to live for God outside of church and also show our devotion to him in the corporate assembly – it's not either/or; each supports the other.

After David's reign, the times of national blessing, victory and security were marked by God-fearing kings reviving Davidic worship. This included King Solomon (2 Chronicles 5-7); Jehoshaphat (2 Chronicles 20); Joash (2 Chronicles 23-24); Hezekiah (2 Chronicles 29-30); Josiah (2 Chronicles 35); Ezra (Ezra 3:10-13); Nehemiah (12:28-46).

So I believe we should not give up meeting together (Hebrews 10:25), but continue to gather for wholehearted music, singing, praise, confession, thanksgiving, prayer, prophesying and creative expressions of worship. And we still need people to lead it, as long as it is holy, loving, and unconditional service to God. That alone is the worship that God desires.

The worship leader that God requires

Now let's take a brief look at the Levites, the tribe of Israel that God set apart to minister to himself, as his royal priesthood. For those who aspire to follow in their footsteps, it is helpful to understand what God specially required of them, our spiritual ancestors. Although we don't read about 'worship leaders' in the Bible, it does refer to the 'chief musicians.'

Contemporary Christian culture has rebranded those key roles as choir director, worship leader, pastor of music and so on. In David's tent sons were under the direction of fathers (and I'm not being gender specific here) with discipleship, training, mentoring, development, activation and release. These are all crucial in growing people and ministers in the house of the Lord.

First of all there were appointments.

Then David spoke to the leaders of the Levites to appoint their brethren to be the singers accompanied by instruments of music, stringed instruments, harps, and cymbals, by raising the voice with resounding joy. So the Levites appointed... (1 Chronicles 15:16-17)

David spoke to the leaders, who appointed those according

to gift and calling. He also recognised those who carried something significant, like Chenaniah, the music master and a leader of the Levites, and three chief musicians, Jeduthan, Asaph and Heman, who were multi-instrumentalists; Asaph the seer was a poet, singer and percussionist.

Personality is often aligned with the call and anointing of God. And we all carry innate gifting and qualities that are released when we minister.

Faithful, available, teachable

These worship leaders were faithful to the call on their lives, and to the king, his captains and elders. They were under authority and not haughty. They were available, setting themselves apart for holy service to the king and his kingdom. They were teachable, able to receive instruction and take direction.

They also knew how to give instruction. David's chief musicians taught others and were leaders, calling the Levites to praise and ordering the ministry in the tabernacle. They took care of the appointments, training and discipleship of the Levites, and there were hundreds of them!

Characteristics of a worship leader

Over thirty-four years' of experience as a worshipper, instrumentalist, worship leader and church pastor, I've trained and mentored worshippers and worship leaders, developed bands, written and arranged songs, produced albums, and led worship for 6-600 people. So I've learned what qualities to look for in those who feel a calling to be a worship leader in the church family:

- **Humble**: this Christ-like attribute is non-negotiable. There is a balance in not thinking too highly of ourselves, or too lowly, either! Understanding our own hearts is part of being humble servant leaders.
- **Teachable**: like the musicians of the tent, we need to be able to take direction, receive instruction and accept

correction under godly authority. An over-confident, know-it-all-all attitude doesn't sit well in the kingdom, and the ability to listen is key to musicianship.

- **Affirmed**: it's vital that we know we are called and chosen by God, because if we are living for the applause of men we will die by their criticism! Healthy encouragement and affirmation is good but the need for accolades cannot eclipse relationship.
- **Serving**: We want people to serve, not to position themselves for promotion, but to care for others. As family we are here to give to each other. Some people only want to be visible and up front, but as part of a team we should be happy to serve and set up too.
- **Loving**: This is the beginning and the end, and applies in three areas of life.
  o **Personal history with God** – no one can have that for you! We must passionately pursue the Lord and invest our hearts in intimacy. Jesus took time with the Father as well as in front of the people. If you can't worship God in your bedroom you'll quickly run out of steam on the platform.
  o **Family relationships** – being a good spouse, parent, son or daughter. We need to love those closest to us and then love those around us, and what happens in the home should also happen in the church family.
  o **Taking care of yourself** – as we're to love our neighbour as ourselves, we must love ourselves and attend to our own heart issues so that the flavour that floods out of us is sweet and not bitter!
- **Releasing**: we must train others to fill our roles and responsibilities if we want growth. Deferring and preferring are essential for development of the younger or the less experienced. We are called to equip those around us.
- **Skilled**: there need to be gifts and skills to work with. When Jesus turned water into wine he started with

something before he transformed it into the finest vintage. Basic musical ability is essential and further skills can be learned.

A worship leader must be a worshipper themselves first, with a heart passionate for Jesus. They need some experience in leading or playing music, knowledge of contemporary worship, a leaning and gifting in leadership, and the more creativity the better! As a worship leader you cannot lead people where you aren't going or where you haven't been yourself.

However, not every worshipper can lead others into the presence of God in worship. Let us explore a little further what kind of 'Levitical' person is required to do that.

Chosen

Out of the world, God chose a people – Israel – to represent him on the earth. Out of Israel, he chose a tribe – the Levites – to represent him to his people and minister to him. Although our focus is on musicians and singers, the Levites were set aside for many roles.

In Moses' time, some were priests, some looked after and transported the tent, others looked after and transported the objects used in the tent, while others prepared the incense and food offerings (Numbers 3 and 4). Some of the priests were judges (Deuteronomy 17:9) and teachers (Deuteronomy 33:8).

In David's time other roles like gatekeepers, watchmen, governors, musicians, treasurers, officials, judges, businessmen and scribes were added (1 Chronicles 9, 25, 26). After the return from exile, the Levites also supervised the rebuilding of the temple (Ezra 3:8-9). The job of a Levite was all to do with providing a place and a means for the people to meet with God in a way he ordained.

God chooses those people...nobody just drifts into it. Nor are the most enthusiastic necessarily the 'chosen ones,' as David learned the hard way (1 Chronicles 13:7-10). Carrying the Ark of the Covenant on a cart like the Philistines did was not God's way.

Good intentions are not necessarily the right way of doing things. His kingly decree said, 'None but the Levites may carry the ark because they were chosen by the Lord to minister before him forever' (1 Chronicles 15:1-2). Likewise, if we are truly concerned for God's honour, we should not seek to lead God's people in worship if we haven't been chosen by him to do so.

Why did God choose the Levites and what is the hallmark of those God chooses for this ministry?

Zealous for God

An event at Mount Sinai transformed the curse of Jacob's prophecy over his angry and violent son, Levi (Genesis 49:5-7), into the blessing of Moses' prophecy over Levi's descendants (Deuteronomy 33:8-11). Moses returned from forty days with God on the mountain receiving the Ten Commandments to find that the Israelites were worshipping a gold calf.

Moses saw that the people were running wild and that Aaron had let them get out of control and so become a laughing stock to their enemies. So he stood at the entrance to the camp and said, 'Whoever is for the LORD, come to me.' And all the Levites rallied to him. Then he said to them, 'This is what the LORD, the God of Israel, says: "Each man strap a sword to his side. Go back and forth through the camp from one end to the other, each killing his brother and friend and neighbour."' The Levites did as Moses commanded, and that day about three thousand of the people died. Then Moses said, 'You have been set apart to the LORD today, for you were against your own sons and brothers, and he has blessed you this day.' (Exodus 32:25-29 NIV)

Because of their zeal for him and his honour, even at the expense of their families and friends, God gave the Levites their place of privilege and responsibility to watch over his word, guard his covenant, teach his people and present offerings for them (Deuteronomy 33:8-11). They alone had the willingness to separate themselves for him, necessary for a life of devotion to him and ministry to his people.

So, the essential characteristic of someone God chooses for this ministry is passion for him above every other thing. If such a cost is too great for us, then we should not seek to serve in the tent of David.

Of a certain age

The Bible sets age limits for those chosen for this ministry. As someone who has just hit his half century, I'm happy to acknowledge that in our modern day we live longer, work longer, and retire later. Still, it's interesting to look at these Old Testament age brackets. The Levites serving in Moses' Tent had to be between 30 and 50 years old (Numbers 4:13). A complementary verse indicates a Levite would begin service at 25 (implying a 5-year apprenticeship) and retire at 50, although he could assist in a small capacity after retirement (Numbers 8:23-26). David lowered the starting age to 20 once the temple was being built in Jerusalem (1 Chronicles 23:24-27). Ezra stuck with this for the rebuilding of the temple and resumption of religious activities following the return from exile (Ezra 3:8-13). These age guidelines could well just be practical wisdom. The ministry of the Levite was a very demanding one that required both maturity and physical strength, and perhaps we should take this principle seriously in the tent of David.

We ought not to rush younger people or allow them to rush themselves into this ministry before they are ready, and even then we should train them for a number of years before they are fully released. And we ought to let and help older people retire with grace and dignity when they can no longer manage the workload this ministry demands.

Consecrated

Before the Levites began service they went through a cleansing ceremony to mark the dedication of the rest of their lives to service in the tent. The priests were ordained by being washed, given new clothes, anointed with oil and blood from a ram sacrificed for their sins and remaining in the tent for seven days (Leviticus 8).

The other Levites were consecrated by being sprinkled with water, shaved all over, having their clothes washed and a bull sacrificed for their sins (Numbers 8:5-14). When David re-commissioned the Levites to bring back the ark accompanied by music, he ordered them to dedicate themselves to this sacred purpose they had been chosen for (1 Chronicles 15:3-14).

The principle is clear. We should not begin leading worship lightly; it must mean a new way of life for us. Just as a marriage or baptismal ceremony publicly mark a decision to end one way of life and begin a new one, something similar may be used for those chosen to lead in the tent of David so they can dedicate themselves before, and to, both God and the church family.

Released

This gives the community the opportunity to acknowledge and support the person in their new life. The Israelites laid hands on the first Levites to recognise God's call on their lives to be their representatives to God and God's representatives to them (Numbers 8:9-10, 16-20). And since there were no part-time Levites they had neither land nor livelihood, so God commanded that the other eleven tribes support them by tithing goods and land (Numbers 18).

The finished work of Jesus means we are all 'priests' and need no other representative between God and us, but again the principle is valuable. Jesus was supported (Luke 8:3) as was Paul (Philippians 4:14-19). The tent of David looks likely to involve 24/7 activity which will need to be facilitated and led by some people. So according to this principle, perhaps eleven families in the church could release one other family to serve full-time?

Skilled

None of us are born with skill. We are born with potential, and we turn aptitude into skill through dedication and practice. Skill is required for those who lead the activities in the tent of David, for example, those appointed to lead in music:

All these men were under the supervision of their fathers for the music of the temple of the LORD, with cymbals, lyres and harps, for the ministry at the house of God. Asaph, Jeduthun and Heman were under the supervision of the king. Along with their relatives – all of them trained and skilled in music for the LORD – they numbered 288. (1 Chronicles 25:6-7 NIV)

There was a lot going on in the tent so they had a lot to learn, to play and prophesy through their instruments (1 Chronicles 25:1), sometimes more than one instrument (1 Chronicles 16:42) for all kinds of songs and selahs. To be able to prophesy in music, to express and accompany God's truth with appropriate sound, implies knowledge of the word of God. They underwent training, usually from their fathers, although it seems David personally trained Asaph, Jeduthun and Heman.

So, should we allow unskilled musicians into our music groups? I think David would say, 'Yes! Anyone chosen by God with sufficient zeal, maturity and strength should be allowed among the musicians, provided they have dedicated their lives to serve in this way. They will become skilful in due course.'

Servant-hearted

Interestingly, despite the apprenticeship system, the chief musicians the fathers and more experienced ones, it seems all the musicians and singers had equal status when ministering in the Tent. For when the time came to sort out the 24-hour rota for the temple:

Young and old alike, teacher as well as student, cast lots for their duties. (1 Chronicles 25:8 NIV)

As for God's people, so for musicians: there is one body

with many parts; each part is indispensable yet dependent on all the other parts. At any one time, some part must lead, but it is a function, not a status. Only loving servants with zeal for God, need apply for service in the tent of David. There are no vacancies for those with big egos!

Conclusion

God will not restore the Tent of David among an unholy people. We don't become holy to worship, we worship to become holy; he is the one who sanctifies us through loving encounter. The true meaning of worship is to set ourselves apart for holy purpose and for God's plan for us. This is the normal Christian life.

When we, the people of God, assemble to minister to him in the 'holy of holies', he also ministers to us. When we come before his presence there is a transference from the holiest of all. This is an expression of our holy way of life and this is what the tabernacle of David is for.

Some from among the people of God should be released to serve in the tent. They are to be dedicated to enabling and leading the assembly in the way God has ordained. Worship truly is a way of life and we are called to live it wholeheartedly.

7

THE 'THANK YOU' THAT REFUSES TO BE SILENCED

Out of the heart the mouth speaks

I have had the opportunity to travel over the years, attending many church meetings, events and conferences. On many occasions I have wondered why it is, at the end of a song in corporate worship, the congregation have nothing to say? There is a gap, not the kind of 'holy silence' I love, the reflective, intimate silence of the contemplative, just an awkward, empty silence.

We have been given so much and released into such freedom; we have been bought with such a price and given eternal significance and eternal life. Is there no offering that we can bring? No thanks on our lips? No praise from the overflow of our heart that would give glory to his name?

More often than not, we don't want to embarrass ourselves, and are bothered about what other people may think. We worry about drawing attention to ourselves (false humility) or want to keep our dignity (pride). Or perhaps we have run out of words.

When Jesus was describing good and bad fruit, he said, *'Out of the overflow of the heart the mouth speaks'* (Luke 6:45). The mouth speaks what the heart is full of! That could be meaningless claptrap or it could be wise, life-giving insights.

There is a beauty of contemplation and intimacy in silence as we connect with our Lord, but the failure to express ourselves freely usually comes from the fear of man. Romans 14 encourages us neither to judge or put obstacles in the way of those whose ways of honouring God are different to our own.

I encourage people to express themselves freely and want to hear what comes out of their mouths, because unlike God, I can't read their hearts. It is when we pray that the heart is revealed. Silent prayer is good when you're alone, but not so helpful when you are gathered to pray together. We need to give the amen of agreement over what we've just prayed about.

Introvert or extravert?

Now of course big groups don't thrill the 40% of quiet introverts in the same way they do the 60% of outgoing extroverts. God was very intentional in designing the intricacies of temperament. But we shouldn't let our personality type or psychological analysis cause us to miss out on his plan. We are wonderfully made and can do all things in Jesus.

What distinguishes extroverts and introverts is where they get their stimulation from. Extroverts get most of it externally, introverts internally. For example, an extrovert tends to process life in company and to find social situations energising; an introvert tends to process alone and to find social situations tiring. Extroverts tend to be energetic and lively and to get things done; introverts tend to be reflective, insightful and to think things through.

Spiritually, the extrovert is attracted to engagement, e.g. worship, celebration, service, fellowship; the introvert is attracted to abstinence, e.g. solitude, silence, simplicity, sacrifice. The extrovert is happy to extend his territory; the introvert is happy to retreat into his. And obviously there are some who are happy in either end of the spectrum.

While an extreme introvert may have no idea how to talk to people, an extreme extrovert may have no idea when to stop talking! Extroverts like to dial up and tap into what's going on around them; introverts like to dial down what's going on outside to tap into what's going on inside of them.

If an extrovert is alone and quiet for too long, they find themselves under-stimulated and bored. If an introvert is in social situations for too long, they become over-stimulated and edgy. I have friends in both of these categories! Certain behaviour is not social ineptness; it is more likely to be design and wiring, which is highly desirable in aspects of creativity, design, science and so on...

I'm not trying to force my preferred style of worship on someone who gets emotional and physical stimulation inwardly. But when we worship corporately, there is a spiritual dynamic we need to be aware of.

Responding in sacrificial obedience to God's instructions means going beyond what comes naturally to us or that which would be considered normal. When we step outside of our comfort zone, we bring something costly to the Lord which can resonate in the atmosphere around us.

'When you hear them sound a long blast on the trumpet, have the whole army give a loud shout; then the wall of the city will collapse and the army will go straight in.' (Joshua 6:5)

The Lord told Joshua that the walls of Jericho would fall with a loud shout. This command wasn't just to the outgoing and aggressive ones; it was to all of the people. It wouldn't have been enough for 60% of the army to shout whilst the quiet ones, the other 40%, contemplated the concept of shouting and missed the moment. God didn't ask for mere mental assent; his battle-winning plan required a loud shout.

'Shout for joy' appears quite a few times in the Psalms. Yes, some find it embarrassing, but when we do as he says, we are operating by his design. He is offering us a transforming moment that can change us from the inside out, and change external situations too. We don't know how it works but when God said, 'Shout!' and his command was followed, the walls fell down.

Personally speaking

I was incredibly shy growing up. When a grown-up spoke to me, I'd manage a smile but little else. As a teenager in a house-group it took me quite a while to say anything at all and I struggled greatly with embarrassment. I wrestled with saying the right thing and getting words out in the right order, but eventually I got comfortable adding what was on my heart into the mix.

It was the same with music. The first time I played percussion in church, I kept my head down and felt there was a massive spotlight on me! I couldn't wait until it was over but somewhere inside I knew this was really important. Thankfully some friends came and encouraged me to raise my voice.

I had to decide whether or not I would believe the lie that I had nothing to say, I couldn't play the drums and I certainly couldn't sing in public. Now many years later on my journey, I'm very comfortable playing, singing or leading gathering! I wonder how many voices we are missing because they have been told they have nothing to add. I would say to them, 'Lift up a shout of praise and silence the lies of the enemy.'

Even though I'd probably score as extrovert, it took some friends' encouragement and the right opportunities for me to step fully into my life's calling. My wife Donna, however, could easily be described as introvert. She doesn't enjoy being at the front hosting a service, preaching or teaching, but as a prophet there is a call on her life to bring the word of God to people.

I so enjoy seeing Donna deliver words of life and truth as we travel, and the way she touches people's hearts is beautiful. She's even run her own school of prophetic ministry and developed some wonderful teaching on how to develop a prophetic culture in church. Every time she stands in front of group it is a personal battle, but she believes in the value of what God has put on her heart and sees the fruit of giving it away.

The truth is we add strength and value to each other when we speak words of hope and promise. Even a simple affirmation or encouragement can transform someone. Sometimes we curtail our freedom of expression out of loving consideration for others worshipping with us. But we don't want to be afraid of expressing ourselves if it would rob others of being inspired, exhorted or comforted in an environment of worship.

The sovereign God of the miraculous knows better than we do. He tells us to give thanks before we have the answer to our questions, lift up praise in readiness to be happy, sing and shout while we are still barren. He is able to do so much more than we could ask or imagine through his power at work in each one of us. Nothing is impossible with God. So let us stretch ourselves in response to his instructions and see what may occur.

And so I encourage you lovely quiet ones to bring what's costly to you in a gathering. Add your voice, which does need to be heard, and adds value to us. And to you outgoing ones, be mindful of those surrounding you, and bring a blessing of encouragement and strength whenever you can.

Heart issues

A good heart should flow with abundance and all of us need to let go of old mind-sets, inhibitions and issues that prevent us from whole-hearted worship. Remember the words of Jesus who said, 'love the Lord your God with all your heart, with all your strength and with all your mind.' Refuse the old ways and choose life.

God said, 'have no other god but me,' (Exodus 20:3). We need to fear the Lord in our hearts and reject any other fear. When we resist the enemy he must flee, so I declare over myself and others, 'Be free in Jesus' name from any spirit of fear, because you are covered by perfect love!'

Repent – literally, change the way you think. Change the way you think about that stuff. Invite Holy Spirit to deal with a rejection issue, fear of failure, unforgiveness or anything that may hold back your heart from loving on purpose.

There is something really freeing and powerful when the church family flows together in vulnerability, in unity and in worship. We inspire and encourage one another. A loud shout or an offering of applause, a flag waved or free movement or a passionate cry, all can spark other flames of passion. Enthusiasm is as just as contagious as apathy!

If we want a vibrant creative culture, then freedom of expression is key. It's got to be real, it's got to be personal, it's got to be passionate and it's got to mean something. He is jealous for us and for our time. He loves us with such an unchanging and furious love that he sent his Son to die for us – he deserves more in return.

Worthy of our worship

Our smart phones are another issue. God wants us present with him, not distracted because you've received a notification, a tweet, a text, a Facebook message, a news report or an email. Unless your sick aunty is just about to die you don't need your phone in your hand during worship. It's all too easy to drift away and start tapping.

My phone lets me communicate with the world. However, if I take my wife out for dinner, I do not spend the precious evening we have together looking at it. Otherwise I would be giving a Facebook update more attention than someone I have a covenant relationship with! She is the one I'm with in that moment, and we have valuable time in a busy week to be together, to enjoy each other's company, to eat good food and to laugh.

In the same way, God is so worth our attention and our focus. He is worthy of our honour and affection. If we want the manifest presence of God, then a little reverence and humility will open the gates for the King of glory to enter in. As we intentionally engage with the journey, let's see what God writes on the letter of our hearts.

Whole-hearted

Whatever is going on, we should be giving what we have to God. We should be happy to pay the price, because he already has. I love to hear people overflowing with the bubbling brook of joy, the roaring thunder of shouting, the quiet whispers of adoration, the heavenly sound of a thousand tongues. The sound we make together changes the atmosphere.

We read in Revelation that worship is going on around the throne all the time, four living creatures, twenty-four elders, myriad angels and a host of the saints worshipping day and night, letting the sweet incense of their worship rise, declaring, 'Holy, holy, holy is the Lord God Almighty, who was and is and is to come. Worthy is the Lamb.'

All of heaven is continuously worshipping the God of glory around the throne, yet we can get bored if we repeat a verse or chorus one too many times! What is going on in our hearts? How can we get restless or weary of giving our heavenly Father our 'thank you'? He has given us everything, yet sometimes we struggle to give him anything.

When facilitating worship, I can't tell the congregation how to worship; I can only encourage them to bring an offering to him. Each one of us needs to look for more, to bring more of ourselves to our gatherings, to come with expectation and with a heart to give rather than just wondering what we might get out of it.

Identity crisis

God deserves the best we have. It's not about how we feel, but about who he is and who we are. We are created in his image and we need an identity check to recognise the likeness of the Lord when we look in the mirror. We are of the bloodline of David and Jesus is our elder brother. We are not only servants, we are all sons and daughters of the Most High God.

That who we represent on the earth and who we are to re-present to the world because we are the brokers of heaven. We're in a distribution business, 'Father & Sons' (and daughters of course!). It's time to come out of the hiding places, to show our faces and reveal the glory on our lives so that the earth where we stand begins to look a lot more like heaven.

Sowing and reaping

There is a kingdom principle at work here called sowing and reaping (2 Corinthians 9:6-11). Praise is the plough for the soil of our hearts. God is not honoured by those who sow sparingly or give grudgingly. He loves to receive the first fruits of our hearts.

He is a God of abundance and loves his children to be like him, abundantly generous and extremely creative. As pretty as pansies are, God is more interested in planting trees, so we have to dig deep. When we walk in his ways, we become like a tree planted by streams of water; we bear fruit and what we do prospers (Psalm 1)! By sowing correctly, we get to reap rich benefits.

The worship of Jesus is an end in itself, not the precursor to the main event. Jesus is the main event! As the shorter Westminster Catechism states, 'The chief end of man is to glorify God and to enjoy him forever.' That mission statement written in 1647 still rings true today and it certainly resonates in my heart.

Glorify God. Do you get it? He has given us everything and he desires an authentic response drawn from our innermost being. Our heartfelt, spontaneous praise is the stuff that attracts his presence. When we encounter our heavenly Father, and meet his unending, unchanging, abounding love for us, our hearts are transformed.

Glory cloud in Pennsylvania

At our Tabernacle of David worship conference, in Pennsylvania, USA, the presence of God was a thick tangible atmosphere in the room. I could sense there was a growing intensity during the worship. We didn't see it at the time, but a photo taken during the joyful celebration shows a cloud hanging above those assembled.

It was a very special event and during the worship we were singing one of my songs. The words of the chorus are:

I cast my crown down at your feet
I fall down, upon my knees and worship you, O holy King
My prayer, my life, my offering...to you, my King.
(from King of the Nations – Alun Leppitt © Ordinary Man Music)

The song is about the awesome splendour of God and how when we offer something valuable to him, we give him the crown of our achievements, laying all that we are at his feet. While we were singing this song, a dancer came slowly and intentionally down the centre aisle, holding aloft a royal purple cushion with gold beading around its edge. On the cushion was a large, gem-encrusted crown.

The dancer's eyes were fixed on the crown that he carefully carried with such regal purpose, as if he was walking up to the throne of the King of Glory himself. I was transfixed as he arrived at the front of the auditorium. He stopped, lowered the cushion, took the crown in his hand, held it high for a moment and just as we were singing the chorus of the song again forcefully threw the crown on the ground and then flung himself to the floor and prostrated himself.

I just about managed to stay on my feet during his powerful sacrifice of praise. It seemed to draw the presence of God closer to us. For me it was a glimpse of what happens before the throne when the twenty-four elders take what is precious and cast it down before the throne of grace. This dancer used the gifts given him to express what was on his heart during that corporate act of worship.

Imagine for a moment if your iPad or other electronic device was a crown. My iPad has a value to me, and I certainly wouldn't throw it violently to the ground. When I lay it down,

I do it carefully so as not to scratch or damage it in any way. The elders' crowns are priceless and they cast them down before the King of kings again and again.

As the dancer offered his stunning display of worship, the hearts of those gathered there responded and a cheer erupted in the room to celebrate King Jesus's majestic presence among us. Then the atmosphere became so intense that one by one the musicians stopped playing as we felt him draw nearer.

I dream of moments like this in worship as everything stopped during the dedication of Solomon's temple, and there in a high school auditorium, it was as if the King of glory had just ridden in. All the band ended up face-down, and the congregation were either kneeling or prostrate before God. I didn't dare move because of the holy presence in that place. There was no sound, no rustling, no agitation, just holy, awesome silence.

After some time, I felt the Lord prompt me with some words of knowledge. His presence was in that place to heal and many were touched around the room as I called out what I could see God doing in the Spirit.

At one point I called out that God was going to heal dyslexia. A young girl at the front responded by picking up the conference brochure and reading it. The normally jumbled letters made sense, and she excitedly told her mother who suggested that she try something a little harder. So she opened her Bible and began to read fluently, saying, 'It makes sense! I can read most of it apart from these names here.' Her mother told her not to worry about the names – no one can read those!

The amazing thing was that after the conference she went home and prayed for her brother who also suffered from dyslexia. He was healed as well! We met them the next day at Our Father's House in Catasauqua and heard the full story from two very excited young people, one receiving in faith through a word of knowledge and then carrying that faith to the other.

All of us in the band were marked forever in that amazing, holy encounter. Our part was making room for what God wanted to do, rather than ploughing along into the next song on the set list. God brought his nature into that place and transformed, healed and delivered people. Sometimes we just need to let go and let God. Rather than figuring out what to do, let's learn how to be.

It's a glory thing

My experience is that when we meet Jesus and see his face, when we glimpse his glory-filled eyes of fire, we are ruined forever. When his wounded hand touches our wounded souls, he restores us. When we drink of the water that Jesus offers us, then living rivers flow from our innermost being. It's unstoppable!

When we invite the Holy Spirit to fill us and lead us, we discover a joy that brings strength in the toughest of times. A fire is ignited in our hearts that will burn for all eternity and we are set forth on a lifetime pursuit of the very best of heaven. All that is within us cries out for more of the consuming fire, all of him covering all of us.

We are just 'earth suits' to be used for his purposes. Arise, shine, bright like a diamond, because the earth will be filled with the knowledge of his glory and our shining will show Jesus to the world. The word knowledge in Habakkuk 2:14 is the Hebrew yada, meaning that the world will be filled with the intimate, experiential knowledge of the glory of the Lord!

There is a reason that jewellers place diamonds on black velvet to show them to prospective customers. Against the darkness, the brightness of the diamonds shines all the more brightly! We are here on earth to rise and shine, revealing the glory of the glorious one through our lives. This is the kind of life worth living. This is real life, not cold and timid, but passionate and full of purpose.

We are called to be worshippers when nobody is watching so that we will know what to do when everybody is watching, and when 'the script has run out.' Overflow of the heart is easy when we have read the truth of the word and soaked in his glory. Choose to stop for a few moments because just one glance from us and he's all over us. Switch off the television for a while, to recharge our spiritual batteries with the 'energia' of Holy Spirit.

Life can be a struggle because of things we go through and issues we face. Even a cursory look at the Psalms shows the questions, dark times, doubt, pain, and suffering within these songs of praise and worship. However there often comes a point that says, 'but I will remember' (Psalm 77:11), 'yet I will praise you' (Psalm 9, 138, 146), and 'wake up, my soul!' (Psalm 57:8). David willed himself to wake up and worship the Lord.

God wants the earth to be filled with his intimate glory and that will happen through us becoming shining ones. We are transformed by divine encounter. As we are touched by the hand of a loving Father, he transforms us from one degree of glory to another. We follow Jesus to become like Jesus, to do the very things Jesus did – and even greater.

Wholehearted

Jesus replied: 'Love the Lord your God with all your heart and with all your soul and with all your mind.' (Matthew 22:37, NIV)

We read in Matthew 22 that Jesus silenced the Sadducees with his astonishing teaching. This Jewish sect didn't believe in resurrection, but had great influence in social, political and religious society, much like the Pharisees, a ruling class in Jewish society who were proud of their own ability to keep the rules. They thought they would trip up the Creator of the universe with their combined wisdom!

Hearing that Jesus had silenced the Sadducees, the Pharisees got together. One of them, an expert in the law, tested him with this question: 'Teacher, which is the greatest commandment in the Law?' Jesus replied: '"Love the Lord your God with all your heart and with all your soul and with all your mind." This is the first and greatest commandment. And the second is like it: "Love your neighbour as yourself." All the Law and the Prophets hang on these two commandments.' (Matthew 22:34 NIV)

Basically, Jesus was saying, 'Love your God with every fibre of your being.'

It is exciting that we get to worship God with everything that we are. At Bridge we get to bring all kinds of creative expressions, not just music and songs but poetry, spoken word, dance, movement, painting and other artistic devotion. We worship with all the grace gifts he has given us.

If it's embarrassing for you to raise your hands in public, raise them anyway. If it costs you something to dance or to do something resembling dancing, then dance like nobody is watching! Dancers, please dance at the front, don't hide at the back. That movement is painting your heart's response on the canvas of our worship. Shout, sing, clap, pray out loud, lie prostrate, kneel, weep: do whatever flows out of your heart to do.

Oil of anointing

Sometimes our worship is like pouring out fine virgin olive oil in an anointed offering for the anointed one. At other times when circumstances have pulled something poignant and powerful from deep within us, what we pour out on Jesus's head is costly perfumed oil like the spikenard of Mary. A sacrifice of praise in the midst of our own loss or pain is a powerful demonstration of being a devoted son or daughter.

Gates of praise

Lift up your heads, O you gates! And be lifted up, you everlasting doors! And the King of glory shall come in. Who is this King of glory? The Lord strong and mighty, the Lord mighty in battle! (Psalm 24:7-8 NKJV)

I want the King of glory to come into our corporate gatherings and take over. I love the outpouring in our meetings because wonderful things happen when Holy Spirit leads the meeting instead of us!

The cry of David in Psalm 24 to the assembly is to 'lift up your heads!' I can imagine him singing, jumping, dancing with all his might, along with his musicians and singers as they returned with the Ark of the Covenant into the ancient city of Jerusalem (2 Samuel 6:12-17). He called for the gates to be flung wide open so that the warrior King might come into the city once again.

David also called out with a loud shout for the heads of the people to be lifted up because the Lord God Almighty is with us. He is our help in times of need, a sure shelter and a mighty tower. Psalm 121 calls for eyes to be lifted up from personal circumstances to focus on the distant mountains because help is on its way. Our help comes from the Lord!

Gates function as protection from the enemy and also to keep things inside. City gates enable the monitoring and control all who enter. In scripture they also represent strength and security; the gatehouses are used for the watchmen on the city walls. But we read that:

The Lord loves the gates of Zion more than all the other dwellings of Jacob. (Psalm 87:2 NKJV)

So the gates of Zion are God's favourite dwelling place. Zion represents the worshipping community and gates are a metaphor for praise. Our praise is the place where God loves to hang out! Isaiah picks up this theme, again calling us to lift up our eyes and look around (verse 4):

But you shall call your walls salvation, and your gates praise. (Isaiah 60:18 NKJV)

Isaiah is describing the prophetic promise over Jerusalem, the spiritual city, another analogy for us as his chosen people. Salvation provides our protection, but the King of glory enters through praise! It breaks something open in the spiritual realm.

In nature a pearl is formed out of irritation, a potentially threatening situation like a parasite inside the oyster shell.

The oyster lays down layers of protection and in doing so forms something valuable and beautiful. The kingdom of heaven is like a pearl of great price, and in Jesus' parable, the merchant sold everything he had to obtain it (Matthew 13:45). The kingdom is worth any price!

Revelation 21:21 says that the twelve gates of the holy city are pearls.

The twelve gates were twelve pearls: each individual gate was of one pearl. And the street of the city was pure gold, like transparent glass. (NKJV)

Each of the gates in the New Jerusalem is made out of one pearl. There he is dwelling in the middle of his people's spontaneous, heartfelt praise.

When we praise God in a place of obstruction and opposition, when we exalt him in the midst of confusion and conflict, when we position ourselves to give him praise in the middle of loss and difficulty, it creates the gate where the King of glory enters in. It forms the pearl of great price in us.

Come in the opposite spirit

When something really hurts us, we need to stop for a moment and give thanks to God. That may be an alien concept to some of us, but it positions us for breakthrough and blessing. Adopting the opposite spirit to the circumstances stacked against us, changes the atmosphere. Then we are able to give him thanks and praise 'at all times in all kinds of situations and circumstances' by declaring something like this:

Father, I give you thanks because you are greater than this situation.
I thank you for your provision and for all you are.
I know you are in charge.
Your mercies and loving kindness are new every single morning.
You are for me and with me always.
Thank you that you never leave or abandon me.

And if you are for me, who can be against me?
I believe that you have set in place everything needed for
my victory.
The battle is yours!
All the honour, praise and thanks belong to you.
I thank you for who you are and who you say I am.
Amen.

Thankfulness prepares you for breakthrough. We all know it's easy to praise God when good stuff happens. When everything is going really well we cheer and celebrate. But, when it seems as though our prayers have not been answered, when we're struggling, when things are difficult and when circumstances cause confusion, that's when the gate is formed in us.

In the hard times it's all too easy for us to drop our heads and take our eyes of the Lord. Self-pity and discouragement will not attract the favour of God. The emotional tricks we try to pull, temper tantrums and crocodile tears, do not move the resources of heaven.

We have to align ourselves with the principles of the kingdom. God is drawn by a heart that is drawn to him; he is captivated by the glance of our eyes (Song of Songs 4:9) and he is attracted to the head that's lifted up. That's why it's so important to 'lift up your heads, O you gates.' So that the King of glory can come in!

Maturity comes at the price of persistence. Through years of suffering chronic illness, I've chosen to persevere, to stay the course and to worship, despite my feelings. I've met my Saviour in the process. Whether or not the answer came in the form I wanted, I have still been determined to love the Lord with everything in me.

I do believe we can draw closer to the one who came near, and in doing so see things from a heavenly perspective. Heaviness lifts off and the anchor of disappointment is cut free and falls to the bottom of the ocean, instead of snagging and dragging along behind me.

While seeking a healing breakthrough, God is worth more to me than the breakthrough, and is always worthy of my praise and thanks. So I activate my faith because I know that without faith it is impossible to please God. Even in a place of challenge, we are comforted to know that Jesus is indeed the author and perfecter of our faith (Hebrews 12:2)!

Lift your heads

Much of what we cry out for in life is only released to us as we lift our heads. It takes more faith to rejoice than it does to hang your head and weep. You are not unworthy. He is worthy and thought you were worth sending Jesus to give his life for yours.

To rejoice, you have to believe you are accepted and favoured by God. Take every difficulty and turn it into praise, because when you do you are forming something God really values – a pearl of great value.

In the community of the redeemed, a gate is the passionate worshippers who lift their heads and declare his greatness. That is what invites the King of glory to come in, the Lord strong and mighty, the Lord mighty in battle! That gate of praise is his favourite dwelling place.

I want the warrior king deep in my heart, in my church, my city and my region. For me that is a 'tabernacle of David.'

8
COSTLY WORSHIP

At the age of twenty-six my health went into crisis. I began losing weight rapidly and was barely able to eat anything without severe abdominal cramps. Eventually I was admitted to hospital and diagnosed with a form of inflammatory bowel disease, ulcerative colitis.

That was the start of years of intense medical treatment, many weeks off work, different types of drugs and surgery to remove the malfunctioning large intestine. For over twenty-four years now, I've dealt with debilitating illness, multiple surgeries, and a suppressed immune system.

It's been so tough to keep going, to keep hoping and to keep trusting. My dear wife Donna has patiently taken the brunt of my frustrations and persistently prayed, in a sacrifice of love! I've been surrounded by friends who have held me up and have leaned into the everlasting arms of the Father. About a year ago, after medical options did little to help my worsening symptoms, I finally consented to an ileostomy.

Over these years bringing anything to the altar has personally cost me. There are many times when my offering has come through pain and confusion, and some of my songs have been written with tears.

Sometimes I could do little more than strum the guitar and sing a few notes, and other times I could only pray and hold on...

Yet God is so kind and gracious. I have known what it is to be kept in the palm of his hand, to find a safe harbour in the storm. He is majestic yet intimately near, awesome, yet I am his friend. All we need is in him. We cannot out-give the generosity of God, who blesses our acts of obedience.

David received prophetic wisdom, counsel and instruction and fulfilled his assignments in a way the Lord found wholly acceptable. After the initial burnt offerings at the dedication of his tent there were no more sacrifices of that type there for thirty-three years, because he knew that God preferred the sacrifice of praise. God will train us in the kingdom lifestyle – generous giving and receiving, thankfulness and gratitude – in other words, worship.

I can testify that worship does shift the mountain of despair, and the darkness that clouds our thinking. The proverb says that hope deferred makes the heart sick. I know what it is to be clinging on with breaking fingernails to faith and desperately hoping that this might be the day everything might change. We have to guard hope and tend our hearts.

My spiritual father Randy Clark gives two compelling talks at his Kingdom Foundations Healing School: 'the thrill of victory' and 'the agony of defeat.' These are powerful, poignant messages about the joy of working miracles and the absolute opposite. It is painful when desperate people come to you and don't get the breakthrough, the answer they are hoping for. I have learnt to remain constant in a place of trust: the Holy Spirit gives us the power to work miracles, but also the power to persevere when the miracles don't come.

In the kingdom we will experience both success and failure and we can still walk in joy. Failure is part of the schooling we need especially when praying for the sick, otherwise we might think we are the ones doing the healing. When we are faithful with whatever we have been given we enter into the Master's joy (Matthew 25:21).

Randy says, 'I'm just the donkey that the King of Glory rides in on.' It is amazing humility from one of our generals of the faith, who has seen hundreds of thousands healed, delivered and saved all over the world.

The problem with chronic pain without the perspective of promise is that it saps your compassion and can cloud your vision. Joy is not the absence of pain but it is the presence of God. We won't find our answers if we focus on the problem, but we will find them in the presence.

Every time I pour my heart out before the throne, regardless of what I feel physically, I know something has changed in me. He refines my heart in the crucible of his love, so I choose to remain open-hearted, expecting the promises to be fulfilled over me, my family and friends. I celebrate when I witness his goodness. Cynicism doesn't work! His peace comes in his presence (peace is joy when it's quiet!)

I have discovered that to have a peace beyond understanding, you sometimes have to navigate through storms in life that you just don't understand! Some of this stuff doesn't line up with our understanding of the Bible. Life really hurts sometimes, yet God is still truly good all the time!

Trust in the Lord with all your heart, and lean not on your own understanding. (Proverbs 3:5 NKJV)

Nothing is too hard for him, because he is faithful.

Faith is more than just believing

James said bluntly, *'faith without deeds is dead'* (James 2:26). Faith is more than doubtlessness or giving mental assent to something; it is real life in action. It is choosing to activate the will because Jesus is worthy, whatever is going on. When our bodies and souls argue back, the Spirit leads and the flesh catches up... eventually! Sometimes it feels like falling back into a waterfall but that waterfall is full of awesome grace.

Trust is the compass and faith the rudder that steers the course. Simple obedience becomes a radical act in times of extreme pain. When I've poured out my devotion and adoration in absolute weakness even while my symptoms are flaring, something beautiful happens. God is truly my God and my time is totally in his hands. Mountains of fear, doubt and despair fall into the sea, and blessed assurance settles every issue of my trembling heart.

Worship that costs us means something to God. It moves heaven's resources and things do change. I haven't yet received the physical healing I've been looking for, but something has been refined in my heart that would not have happened any other way. God is so good that I soon run out of superlatives!

In costly worship fear leaves, heart attitudes adjust, life gets re-calibrated by love. And often it touches the people around you too.

Vision of Jesus

Once I was facing an emotional battle that I lacked the energy to fight. In a small gathering of friends, while we waited on the Lord, the tempo of my heart changed as I sensed the louder rhythm of heaven's heartbeat pulsing through. In a moment of encounter, I had a vision that undid me, chased away the demons and left me feeling light and released.

In my vision, I was on my knees, doubled over in anguish and weeping. I had travelled on a long winding path and before me was a mountain that seemed like a towering shadow. Having journeyed so far I didn't have the strength to climb any more. But the steady, assured beating of heaven's drum told me to lift me head.

My tears stopped and I slowly lifted my gaze. At the top of the mountain I saw one enormous foot and then another; my gaze continued upwards and there, standing astride the mountain was Jesus! He was like a superman, with sunlight glowing around his head, almost too bright to look upon. He was enormous, standing confident, powerful and full of strength.

I was stunned by the revelation unfolding before my eyes and the words, 'Let the weak say, "I am strong,"' came to mind. The reality is that Jesus had already conquered that summit and beckoned me on. In his strength I could continue. I spent some time resting in his refreshing and felt my spirit being renewed.

I picked up a pen and wrote:

You stand astride the insurmountable
You dominate my horizon with faithfulness
Your face shines glorious with favour
Your smile radiates like the sun
The warmth of your love dissipates every doubt
As the light of the Son burns away the morning mist of confusion...
You are faithful and true.

We need to see Jesus magnificent and towering over anything that overshadows us. He has indeed overcome the world. Jesus knows no impossibility, which makes the impossible possible for us! So I encourage you to bring your heart again to Jesus in intimacy and vulnerability and pour out an offering. Let him have his way in you.

I will praise you, LORD, with all my heart; I will tell of all your wonderful deeds. I will be glad and rejoice in you; I will sing the praises of your name, O Most High. (Psalm 9:1-2 NIV)

I will praise you with my whole heart; before the gods I will sing praises to you. I will worship toward your holy temple, and praise your name, for your lovingkindness and your truth; for you have magnified your word above all. In the day when I cried out, you answered me, and made me bold with strength in my soul. All the kings of the earth shall praise you, O Lord, when they hear the words of your mouth. Yes, they shall sing of the ways of the Lord, for great is the glory of the Lord. (Psalm 138:1-5 NKJV)

House of peace

People who come into my home often talk about how peaceful it feels. They are picking up on something that has been established in the spiritual realm and manifested in our home. Worship releases something that lasts more than just a moment; it opens the way for incredible encounters with the Holy Spirit.

Now thanks be to God who always leads us in triumph in Christ, and through us diffuses the fragrance of his knowledge in every place. For we are to God the fragrance of Christ among those who are being saved and among those who are perishing. (2 Corinthians 2:14-15 NKJV)

Under the shadow of his wings is a place of healing and authority so that we can carry the fragrance of the God everywhere we go. Many of us fix onto something insubstantial and then get cast adrift on emotional highs and lows. God wants us to anchor our affections in the world we cannot see, the Kingdom of God.

The fear of God is an absolute trembling in his presence. There will be times in the very near future when we will become aware that the Lord God Almighty, the commander of angelic armies, the God of all might and strength, has just stepped into the room. There may not be many left standing, but his glory will rest upon us in ways we have not yet experienced.

I have tasted those moments and I long for more. I long to drink from those kind of waters again so that praise will roar loudly once again from my heart! Costly worship is powerful to bring release, break chains, set captives free and bring salvation.

I will not give the Lord that which costs me nothing

In 2 Samuel 24 we read how David took a census of his people and violated a specific command of God. The captain of his army, Joab, tried to persuade David to change his mind, but he didn't listen. In pride he wanted to know how great he was in number, but this sin had consequences for the nation; a pestilence was sent as a result of the Lord's wrath and 70,000 died.

When David saw what was going on he went and pleaded with God to stop. Even in his flawed nature, he stood as a forerunner of Jesus, saying, 'Let the punishment be on my head. Let me take the blame, not them.' The difference, of course, was that David was clearly to blame and Jesus was innocent.

The prophet Gad came to David and assigned him to perform an offering on Araunah's threshing floor. Araunah wanted to give the king the place to build his altar as a gift, but David would not, and could not, make an offering that way. His desire was to make an offering acceptable to the Lord.

But the king replied to Araunah, 'No, I insist on paying you for it. I will not sacrifice to the Lord my God burnt offerings that cost me nothing.' So David bought the threshing floor and the oxen and paid fifty shekels of silver for them. (2 Samuel 24:24 NIV)

He created the altar, made his sacrifice, and the plague was averted from the nation.

David could have come to Arunah and demanded the threshing floor. But if he had done, that it would have been like Cain's half-hearted offering, which did not please God. The Lord wants the offering of Abel, the first fruits of our heart. He wants the best, the excellence of our hearts.

In every aspect of our lives we give to God first before we do anything else. This is especially important with our finances. In a life of grace we can miss the crucial importance of kingdom principles like sowing and reaping. Things we offer the Lord should be significant.

'I will not give the Lord that which costs me nothing.'

That phrase has become the hallmark of my life. I believe in healing and have had the privilege of seeing hundreds of people healed, but have still not received that healing I so desperately need in my own body. I have purposed in my heart to follow him whatever the cost, knowing that others have paid a far higher price in sacrifice and devotion than I have.

'What I have vowed'

Jonah was a prophet of the Lord with a simple assignment, though maybe not an easy one. All he had to do was obey the Lord, but he chose to run away.

Now the word of the Lord came to Jonah the son of Amittai, saying, 'Arise, go to Nineveh, that great city, and cry out against it; for their wickedness has come up before Me.' But Jonah arose to flee to Tarshish from the presence of the Lord. He went down to Joppa, and found a ship going to Tarshish; so he paid the fare, and went down into it, to go with them to Tarshish from the presence of the Lord. (Jonah 1:1-3 NKJV)

Jonah should have known that you can't flee from the omniscient one, but tried anyway, and God sent a violent storm to shake him out of his disobedience. As the wind rose and massive waves crashed into the boat, the sailors, normally a superstitious lot, tried to work out why such a storm should have beset them.

They eventually woke Jonah and called on him to pray to his God to help. The sailors cast lots and the lot fell to him so he had to own up that he was running away from the Lord of heaven and earth, maker of the seas and the skies. In a noble moment Jonah told them to throw him overboard so that the storm would be calmed and they would be saved.

They were terrified and tried to row back to land, but the storm grew even wilder than before and so they asked God for forgiveness and chucked Jonah over the side!

Sure enough the winds died down, the sea grew calm and they were rescued from certain death in the terrible storm.

At this the men greatly feared the LORD, and they offered a sacrifice to the LORD and made vows to him. But the LORD provided a great fish to swallow Jonah, and Jonah was inside the fish three days and three nights. (Jonah 1:16-17)

This was an unusual lifeboat!

It must have been rank inside the fish and after three days Jonah must have thought it would only be a short while before the digestive juices dissolved him completely.

In that dark pit, Jonah threw himself onto the Lord's everlasting mercy.

Then Jonah prayed to the Lord his God from the fish's belly. And he said: 'I cried out to the Lord because of my affliction, and he answered me. Out of the belly of Sheol I cried, and you heard my voice. For you cast me into the deep, into the heart of the seas, and the floods surrounded me; all your billows and your waves passed over me. Then I said, "I have been cast out of your sight; yet I will look again toward your holy temple."

'The waters surrounded me, even to my soul; the deep closed around me; weeds were wrapped around my head. I went down to the moorings of the mountains; the earth with its bars closed behind me forever; yet you have brought up my life from the pit, O Lord, my God.

'When my soul fainted within me, I remembered the Lord; and my prayer went up to you, into your holy temple. Those who regard worthless idols forsake their own mercy. But I will sacrifice to you with the voice of thanksgiving; I will pay what I have vowed. Salvation is of the Lord.' (Jonah 2:1-9 NJKV)

It was a prophetic promise to the Lord, 'yet I will look toward your holy temple and with a song of thanksgiving I will sacrifice to you.' Even as Jonah thought he faced his last breath, he said, 'What I have vowed, I will make good.'

And the LORD commanded the fish, and it vomited Jonah onto dry land. (Jonah 2:10 NKJV)

The God of second chances told Jonah again to deliver the message to Nineveh, and this time he was obedient. So probably a little the worse for wear, bleached by stomach acid, dishevelled and smelling of 'Eau de whale,' Jonah delivered the word of the Lord and the whole city, including the king, repented before God.

When God saw what they did and how they turned from their evil ways, he had compassion and did not bring upon them the destruction he had threatened. (Jonah 3:10 NKJV)

Peace be with you...and also with you!

So Jonah's worship not only set him free, but it delivered 120,000 people from destruction. There are echoes of David's psalms in Jonah's prayer. God responds to our hearts. We are responsible for what flows out of our hearts, and encouraged to guard them.

And the peace of God, which transcends all understanding, will guard your hearts and your minds in Christ Jesus. (Philippians 4:7 NIV)

We must rest in peace! Not dead, but resting in a peace beyond our understanding. God wants us to operate from a place of peace, not striving or anxiety.

Leif Hetland said recently, 'God wants to bless the *rest* of your life.' So we work from a place of rest, not having to rest from all of our work! Rest and peace are perfectly intertwined. Peace can enable us to sleep through a storm and carry the kind of authority and grace that Jesus did. We can release that peace in a room without even knowing it and change the atmosphere around us, just as Peter's shadow released what overshadowed him (Acts 5:15).

Shalom is a powerful word, pregnant with promise. When believing believers say it to a friend, enemy, shopkeeper or anyone at all, we are releasing the promise of his peace in us, onto them. It is everything as it should be, over you and in you. It is his completeness, prosperity and wellbeing in your circumstances, in Jesus' name.

Jailhouse rock

In Acts 16 we read of Paul and Silas preaching in Macedonia. They had seen people converted when they went along by the river near Philippi, but were being hassled by a slave girl who could foresee the future...

This girl followed Paul and us, and cried out, saying, 'These men are the servants of the Most High God, who proclaim to us the way of salvation.' And this she did for many days. But Paul, greatly annoyed, turned and said to the spirit, 'I

*command you in the name of Jesus Christ to come out of her.'
And it came out that very hour.* (Acts 16:17-18)

Even though the demonised girl was announcing what their mission and mandate was, Paul cast out the demon. Her owners weren't best pleased because the fortune-telling spirit was now gone, and their money-making scheme was ruined. So they dragged Paul and Silas off, got them arrested, and the local magistrates ordered them to be stripped and beaten.

And when they had laid many stripes on them, they threw them into prison, commanding the jailer to keep them securely. Having received such a charge, he put them into the inner prison and fastened their feet in the stocks. But at midnight Paul and Silas were praying and singing hymns to God, and the prisoners were listening to them. (Acts 16:23-25 NKJV)

Now, if I met someone spouting stuff about the future, eyes rolling and mouth frothing, I'd probably want to offer some spiritual cleansing. If I was then beaten and thrown into jail on trumped-up charges I might well moan about the unfairness of it all while nursing my bruises.

But Paul and Silas knew the power of praise and worship, and though beaten they were not broken in spirit. So in the most secure cell of the jail, guarded and chained to the floor in heavy fetters, they rocked. They knew in whom they trusted, so instead of whimpering, they held a worship service to the Most High God. Shrugging off their circumstances they released prayers and petitions.

In Isaiah 61 the Lord says, 'Heaven is my throne, and the earth is my footstool.' And I imagine God looking down from his throne room at his faithful followers worshipping with all their might in extraordinary adversity, and tapping his feet to the jailhouse rock. Paul and Silas kept pressing in until midnight when something extraordinary happened:

Suddenly there was a great earthquake, so that the foundations of the prison were shaken; and immediately all the doors were opened and everyone's chains were loosed.

133

And the keeper of the prison, awaking from sleep and seeing the prison doors open, supposing the prisoners had fled, drew his sword and was about to kill himself. But Paul called with a loud voice, saying, 'Do yourself no harm, for we are all here.' (Acts 16:26-28 NKJV)

So the jailer rushed in with his torch, and in fear and trembling asked, 'What must I do to be saved?' That doesn't happen much in our worship services! Yet, there in a dank, dark prison cell, the fear of the Lord came upon this man and he fell on the Lord's mercy.

So they said, 'Believe on the Lord Jesus Christ, and you will be saved, you and your household.' Then they spoke the word of the Lord to him and to all who were in his house. And he took them the same hour of the night and washed their stripes. And immediately he and all his family were baptised. Now when he had brought them into his house, he set food before them; and he rejoiced, having believed in God with all his household. (Acts 16:31-34 NKJV)

Costly worship for Paul and Silas resulted in a supernatural event with angelic assistance. The jailor and his family were saved, he cleansed their wounds and fed them, and they were released from prison the next day. So their wholehearted worship set them free from captivity; what started in pain and darkness ended with freedom, salvation and favour.

Public declarations of spontaneous praise can be accompanied by spectacular results that cause people to seek him and provide us with the opportunity to tell them about him. Perhaps we need to take our praise, worship and prophetic music out into the streets and see what God does!

I sense this is the time to release a fresh sound outside of our churches. It will be the sound of deliverance, the sound of salvation, the sound of mercy and the sound of war as we destroy the works of the enemy with guitar, drum and voice.

Jesus shows us through his own life the path we need to take. It will cost us our pride, our fear of man, our indecision and our right to say no to God. In that single-minded pursuit there is freedom like no other and a peace that calms every storm. Such worship in spirit and truth will bring heaven on earth.

The fragrant offering

Let's look at a beautiful moment that happened in the week leading up to the crucifixion. (See also Matthew 26:6-13 and Mark 14:3-9).

Then, six days before the Passover, Jesus came to Bethany, where Lazarus was who had been dead, whom he had raised from the dead. There they made him a supper; and Martha served, but Lazarus was one of those who sat at the table with him. Then Mary took a pound of very costly oil of spikenard, anointed the feet of Jesus, and wiped his feet with her hair. And the house was filled with the fragrance of the oil.

But one of his disciples, Judas Iscariot, Simon's son, who would betray him, said, 'Why was this fragrant oil not sold for three hundred denarii and given to the poor?' This he said, not that he cared for the poor, but because he was a thief, and had the money box; and he used to take what was put in it.

But Jesus said, 'Let her alone; she has kept this for the day of my burial. For the poor you have with you always, but me you do not have always.' (John 12:1-8 NKJV)

This is Mary who sat at Jesus' feet instead of fussing in the kitchen (Luke 10:38). As she turned all her attention on Jesus, she gave a very costly gift to thank Jesus for the way he had touched her life. He accepted and received this extravagant offering.

Mary broke the neck of the expensive jar; it would never be used again. Then she poured and poured this highly perfumed oil over Jesus' head and wiped his soon-to-be nail-pierced feet with her hair. The whole house was filled with fragrance, and Mary herself would have been covered in the same oil she anointed Jesus with.

When extravagant worship overflows from our heart to his, and we bow towards our Saviour, it is a fragrant offering, so acceptable to him. He defends us from the hostile reactions of others and he receives our sweet gift. He knows when we pour ourselves out that we will be changed in the process. Every time we embrace Jesus, the anointed one, his exquisite fragrance rubs off on us.

There was nothing in the world like the holy anointing oil described in Exodus 30. Extravagant ingredients – 500 shekels of this, 250 shekels of that, and so on – were all brought together with great skill and care. It had a holy purpose because whatever the oil touched was made holy and whatever touched them became holy too. So in the outer court where grace was shown, in the Holy Place where God was served and in the Holy of Holies where God was seen in his glory, all the tabernacle was filled with the fragrance of this holy anointing oil.

God still wants the fragrance of mercy, love and kindness to be all around. He wants the sweet perfume of sacrifice and worship to be carried by his people. Just as Aaron and the priests were anointed and consecrated, so are we anointed for a holy purpose. Christ is the smeared one, the anointed one, the 'ointment poured forth.' He gave his life to us so we can carry that aroma of Christ everywhere we go.

When is it too much?
We may struggle with excess, but Jesus didn't. He loved what Mary did for him in Bethany, even when his companions thought it was excessive or wasteful. Jesus received the free and open way Mary poured out herself out to him. Her lavish offering was priceless, personal and intimate.

There was a battleground over that sacrifice of praise. Judas sharply criticised Mary, already calculating what he could have taken out of the sales of this valuable commodity, Jesus told him to let her alone – her act of worship was also an anointing for burial. Mary had an insight into who Jesus was and what he had come for, that these disciples didn't. They were indignant and didn't really get it – they should have been called the 'duh'-ciples!

The enemy tried to rob Mary of her personal worship, but Jesus protected her, saying that everywhere the Gospel will be preached she would be remembered. This was the most costly act of physical worship done to Jesus. The finest spikenard, worth a year's wages, was poured out over the Saviour of the world.

Don't judge

'Don't judge or you will be judged,' said Jesus. We live in an X-Factor culture where everyone gets judged on looks, style, tuning, ability and very rarely their heart. But grading performance is not appropriate in worship. We can feel exposed and vulnerable, so let us choose to honour and love one another with a gentle kindness. Calling out the gold in one another's hearts is so much more pleasing to Jesus than criticism and contempt.

To worship is to be changed

There is an exquisite heavenly equation in worship. Even though it is for God, it changes us. God's looking for each one of us to become a worshipper, because in that place of overflow we are transformed. Our heavenly Daddy knows that when we hang around Jesus, we will become like that which we behold.

So come and behold him. The invitation is before us: 'Seek my face, seek my presence.' And our heart's response is, 'Your face, Lord, I will seek!' In that place a costly fragrance is released which we carry with us everywhere.

9
PUNCHING HOLES AND DIGGING WELLS

The invitation to conquer

I wrote this chapter in Italy with a majestic view of Lake Como reflecting the scudding clouds and the range of stunning, snow-topped mountains. The mountains draw forth a primeval instinct to climb, to get to the top of that summit and see the view, to conquer something so grand and imposing. It calls out the deeper desire in me for greatness, to dare greatly, to try, and even fail while trying.

We are here for a divine purpose and the mountain speaks to me of vision. When you have a vision for something, you put plans in place, make provision and train. I couldn't scale that mountain wearing a pair of shorts and trainers on my feet!

King David had two attempts at returning the Ark of the Covenant to Jerusalem. After the first one ended in disaster and the death of his helping hands (2 Samuel 6), he put some plans in place before making second attempt at the summit. The peak of his vision was to restore the representation of God's presence to its rightful place in the centre of his gathered people.

So three months later with a great procession of musicians, singers and great rejoicing, they came back into the city with the Levites carrying the Ark the ordained way. David's queen Michal was offended when he danced, but that offence left her barren. Pride, bitterness, resentment and unforgiveness all block us from blessing. As for David, he defiantly declared that he would become even more undignified before the Lord.

Obstacles and opposition

The mountain, resplendent in its cloak of cloud challenges me, 'How high do you want to go?' We all want to go to the top, until we face obstacles! Then we question whether God really told us to go; our vision becomes confused and the path that once seemed clear is obscured. Sometimes it's a long road to the place you are called to, but I have discovered that God's delays are not God's denials.

Isaiah said: *'I have set my face like flint and I know that I will not be ashamed'* (Isaiah 50:7 NASB). There are times we need to press on in, to break through into a new and spacious place, a new landscape. Whether we believe it or not, we are in a war! Our enemy opposes us, wanting to steal from us and kill off our hope, faith and love.

I have scars from a motorbike accident that potentially could have killed me and my daughter. A car pulled in front of us at nearly 30mph, and we went flying over its bonnet and into the road. The bike was a complete write-off, yet there wasn't a scratch on my jacket or crash helmet. It seems that an angel came to soften our fall – thank you, Jesus.

Is this life scary? Not really, if you know who you are and who your God is! Jesus said, *'The thief comes only to steal and kill and destroy. I came that they may have life and have it abundantly'* (John 10:10 NASB). Therefore anything that is not abundant life is not from God.

Some have created a skewed theology about sickness and disease being for our character development, perhaps to justify our lack of power. The miraculous signs and gifts were given to accompany the Great Commission (Mark 16:17-18, Acts 4:29-30) and to build up the church (1 Corinthians 12:7-10). To deny them falls desperately short of the promise, the plan and the purpose of our lives.

We are here to conquer the impossible, because we are connected to him who knows no impossibility! Whatever the circumstances, God is for us and is with us to vindicate us. The Lord God Almighty, the really big and really strong God – that's our Daddy! The one who overcame the world, disarmed the enemy and made a public spectacle of him is our awesome, glorious Jesus.

Punching holes

Several years ago I took a team of worshippers from Bridge to a church in Graz, Austria. The church had been persecuted in the local press with lies written and spoken about them. There was vehement opposition from local authorities to use certain premises so they had to move to another part of town to hold their meetings. Numbers had declined, there were financial difficulties and the pastors had voluntarily taken a salary reduction to keep the church afloat.

However, by prayer and pressing through, something was shifting for them. We were invited to come and join in an evening of 'spiritual warfare.' For us that meant worship and celebration. It's 'joy-fare,' not warfare – if you don't enjoy it, you're not doing it right! Not striving, but flowing with what God is doing and declaring the Name above all names, King Jesus.

We gathered on a cold, cloudy day in the same venue that the church had been hounded out of some years previously. The distant mountains that surrounded this town were barely visible and the atmosphere felt heavy and oppressive. As we prayed, we had a wild, Holy Spirit-fuelled time with laughter, joy and some intense moments too. Like many of us I ended up on the floor just soaking in the presence, but while I lay there God spoke to me quite profoundly.

I suddenly had an amazing vision of being deep in a forest. Birds were singing and shafts of sunlight were spotlighting the soft forest floor when out from a group of trees a mighty, dark-maned lion appeared. Surprisingly, I felt so peaceful, because I knew it was Jesus – the Lion of the tribe of Judah. I have many lion paintings and sculptures in my house, so I love it when God speaks to me in this way.

I felt Jesus say, 'Get up, Alun, it's time to do battle.' I asked him, 'Will you be with me,' and he said, 'I am with you always.' I immediately sat up, wondering why I asked Jesus that question when he had already defined that truth for all time in scripture, and thought, 'Why didn't I ask for a great strategy to overcome the enemy's scheme? Why didn't I ask for a song to change the world?'

The fact is that I knew the answer in my head, but when Jesus, the lion spoke to me, it had such substance. It strengthened my resolve and gave me great courage. It was very, very powerful. God knows exactly what we need to hear in any given moment and 'I am with you always' was what I needed to hear on that floor in Austria. There is something quite profound when the great 'I AM' says this directly to your heart!

That word perfected my courage, and my desire to declare the name of Jesus and release faith for anything to happen during the celebration evening. It certainly was amazing as worship teams from two congregations and friends from other churches joined together in one spirit to worship wholeheartedly and declare prophetic decree.

I have felt for many years there was a special grace on us as a team to 'punch holes' in spiritual atmospheres when we worship. Well, the prince and the power of the air got his face well and truly punched in that night! We didn't shout much, other than in praise. We certainly paid no attention to the dark side; our battle was to glory in and glorify Father, Son and Holy Spirit.

In his kindness, God's manifest presence was thick that evening. We declared truth from scripture, gave prophetic pictures and words and worshiped our heads off! He poured out his love on us, soaked us through and through, and many were left trembling in his glory. I think we laughed a lot too.

Alex, a member of the band, saw a vision of a large demonic figure standing looking at what was going on. While we were engaging in our warfare a long, javelin-like spear was thrown towards it and it turned to run but the spear pierced the centre of its back and it disappeared. Alex felt that whatever force was opposing the church was removed by our unified praise and worship.

When we left at the end of the night, the sky was so huge and bright, I felt I could see into the heavens; the moon was luminescent with the stars pin-sharp. Around us the mountains were clearly visible. The cloud cover had disappeared from above us and there was a hole in the sky revealing the shining stars, a clear sign of the warfare that had just taken place in the heavenly realm.

As I stood there I was back in my vision again, but this time the Lion was just behind me. I didn't turn around; I just knew he was there, and he spoke into my heart: 'Well done, Alun, you fought well tonight.' Jesus had come back to encourage and strengthen me. That was a huge confirmation of what I had felt for so long.

The Lion's roar

In the Chronicles of Narnia film, Prince Caspian, there is an amazing scene of Lucy standing tiny and alone on a bridge. Her only weapons are the fledgling bravery in her heart breathed into existence by Aslan, and a tiny dagger in her hand. Yet she stands willing to fight the might of the Telmarine army swarming to the bridge. Her valiant faith reveals Aslan himself, and when this lion roars, a powerful shockwave detonates in the earth and scatters the enemy.

There is something about standing firm after having done everything we know to do. We must stand on the truth, stand on the rock. And there is also something about the roar of the worshipper's heart. Our praise and worship change what is happening in the spiritual realm and bring confusion and devastation to the enemy's camp (2 Chronicles 20).

Jesus is described as the Lion of the tribe of Judah (Revelation 5:5). Judah is the Hebrew (yehudhah) for praised and it was the wholehearted tribe of Judah who were the first among the worshippers and first into battle. David and the ultimate prophet, priest and king, Jesus, were descendants of Judah. Our praise of the Lord God is a powerful act of submission. And the lion's roar is heart cry of a laid-down lover that Jesus is Lord and his kingdom has come!

In scripture the lion is sometimes the good guy (Proverbs 28:1), and sometimes the bad guy (Psalm 57:4), representing God (Amos 3:8) or Satan (1 Peter 5:8). But overall, it is a biblical metaphor for courage, authority and ferocity, and one of the many metaphors Jesus is happy to have associated with him.

We are in a battle and are summoned to be overcomers. In Revelation 5 we find a scroll, and the only one found worthy to open it is the conquering Lion of the tribe of Judah, the Root of David. But as we focus on the lion, we find a slaughtered lamb instead. The four living creatures and the twenty-four elders recognise the lamb as the all-conquering hero, and fall before him in worship. They are soon joined in doing so by all the hosts of heaven.

The power of God expressed by a slain lamb encapsulates the gospel. To overcome like Jesus is to do so with lamb-like sacrificial love, not with roaring violence. Almighty God became a vulnerable baby, and the king of the Jews took on the role of a servant. The messianic Lion of Judah defeated all his enemies as the sacrificial lamb of Calvary. So Jesus showed that the most powerful force in the universe is courageous servanthood and sacrifice.

Worship is an act of war

There is an intrinsic link between obedience and humility to release God's favour and power. As we worshipped, God sent his angel armies to do battle for us. Spiritual forces in the heavenly realms heard the wisdom of the God through the saints and left – resist the enemy and he must flee! And our praise resisted every plan of the enemy to oppose God's people in that place. Under that clear sky I felt a peace and lightness.

The following Sunday the church was full. A visiting speaker felt prompted to take a special offering for the church after the usual offering taken during the service. The church leaders would never normally do this but over €13,000 was given, many times the normal amount! God moved in incredible ways in that church and in their young people in the months that followed. A hole was punched into the spiritual realm through an act of war – our obedient worship.

Jesus took on human form so that the works of the devil would be destroyed (1 John 3:8). The son of God became the Son of Man, so that the sons of men would become sons of God. We sons and daughters now get to carry on the family business: destroying the works of the enemy! That is our great enterprise.

Digging wells

In Abraham's day water represented life. Wells were dug by hand with much hard labour through solid limestone, sometimes with steps carved in the wall for people to descend, or ropes and buckets or water-skins to draw the water out. Wells were vital to the herdsmen in this desert country; without them they could not exist. Those who owned them sold their water, or bartered with those who used the well, so they generally became important men in the land.

Abraham was a wealthy man with many possessions, flocks herds and servants and he passed his wealth and knowledge onto his son Isaac. In Genesis 26 we read of a great famine gripping the land. Isaac decided to go to Gerar, towards King Abimelech of the Philistines. On the way the Lord spoke with Isaac.

'Isaac, stay away from Egypt! I will show you where I want you to go. You will live there as a foreigner, but I will be with you and bless you. I will keep my promise to your father

Abraham by giving this land to you and your descendants. I will give you as many descendants as there are stars in the sky, and I will give your descendants all of this land. They will be a blessing to every nation on earth because Abraham did everything I told him to do.' (Genesis 26:2-5 CEV)

God confirmed to Isaac the promise made to his father, 'your descendants will be a blessing to every nation.' Isaac was familiar with God's voice, his nature and his ways, and followed in his father's footsteps, displaying radical obedience in the face of famine and the unknown. Obedience to God releases blessings. His words speak life into any famine and his breath revives dry bones.

So Isaac dwelt in Gerar, a Philistine district in south central Israel with his wife Rebekah. As he followed the Lord's guidance he planted grain. Sowing seed in difficult times is an act of faith, and the harvest gave a hundredfold increase (Genesis 26:12). The Lord blessed Isaac just as he promised.

God loves to shower us with his abundant goodness. In our church fellowship, as we bless one another and are radically generous, he breaks the crisis of debt, brings release from hardship and transforms our circumstances. When breakthrough comes, it changes the way we think about the goodness of God.

Before the breakthrough

Sometimes before the breakthrough, there is contesting. There is dispute over the land and there is pressure. But God positions us for breakthrough.

As God prospered Isaac in everything he did, his possessions increased, as did his flocks, herds and servants. He became very great in the land. King Abimelech felt threatened and asked him to move on, so he went into the valley and re-dug the wells that the Philistines had filled in. God placed him in the land he knew from his childhood and there must have been great joy in the camp as they struck fresh running waters.

This story resonates in my heart as God moves in the

nations, especially in the places of historic revival. I believe there is a call on the people of God to re-dig wells as well as to dig new ones. There are wells of salvation waiting to have the water drawn out of them again. And the water will be drawn with great rejoicing (Isaiah 12:3).

As Isaac and his servants re-dug his father's wells, the local herdsman claimed the water for themselves. Isaac moved and dug another well, but the ground was contested again as the locals again claimed the water as their own. A third time Isaac moved his flocks, herds and servants and dug another well. This time the ground was not quarrelled over and Isaac named the place Rehoboth, which literally means 'spacious place' (Genesis 26:22).

Isaac named the place where he would pitch his tent and decreed that they would be fruitful in the land. He had seen the hand of God make room for him and believed in the promise spoken over his life. As we decree a thing, we see it established.

That is what we are here to do: speak the truth of God's promises and see circumstances change. Interestingly Isaac didn't stay and fight over the first or the second well, he simply moved on. When there was contestation he simply dug another well, trusting in the promise of God. He knew the importance of water for his family and animals and did what was necessary in an attitude of peace. When the third well was dug he found it to be the perfect, spacious place.

Then he went up from there to Beersheba. And the Lord appeared to him the same night and said, 'I am the God of your father Abraham; do not fear, for I am with you. I will bless you and multiply your descendants for my servant Abraham's sake.' So he built an altar there and called on the name of the Lord, and he pitched his tent there; and there Isaac's servants dug a well. (Genesis 26:23-25 NKJV)

The promise God made with Abraham was once again reaffirmed to Isaac. Isaac had a place of rest and peace in his heart because of the living promise over his life. He walked in the assurance of God's sustaining word for him and his descendants. Even in the face of opposition he trusted God implicitly for provision, wells of wealth, blessing and salvation.

What happened next is remarkable: Abimelech sought him out. Isaac might have assumed that more trouble was coming.

And Isaac said to them, 'Why have you come to me, since you hate me and have sent me away from you?' But they said, 'We have certainly seen that the Lord is with you. So we said, "Let there now be an oath between us, between you and us; and let us make a covenant with you, that you will do us no harm, since we have not touched you, and since we have done nothing to you but good and have sent you away in peace. You are now the blessed of the Lord."'

So he made them a feast, and they ate and drank. Then they arose early in the morning and swore an oath with one another; and Isaac sent them away, and they departed from him in peace. (Genesis 26:27-31 NJKV)

An amazing peace agreement was made between the Philistines and Isaac, the same day his servants found the water. Isaac named the place Beersheba, the place of seven wells, the well of a sevenfold oath. He lived in the promise, which brought about a peace that lasted his lifetime.

Set about digging...

For a season our church met in the old sanctuary of Central Baptist church in Southampton. Like other places in the UK, Southampton has geothermal springs and several well heads including an old one very near this church. The city geothermal project heats almost 20% of the district, bringing heating to our civic centre, central housing and shopping mall.

Following a visit to Toronto in 2003 our prayer was, 'Lord, if you can move there, you can move here in our city.' We had heard so many testimonies of what God was doing all over the earth as a result of people who had sought the Lord at Catch the Fire, Toronto. So we positioned ourselves for blessings, prayed and decreed and began to dig a well of revival, healing and worship in Southampton.

Over a decade ago churches in our locality barely discussed healing, yet we hosted significant healing conferences and trained and equipped teams to pray and minister to the sick. Cal Pearce, international director of the Healing Rooms came for a national conference in 2005 in Central Baptist Church and this event brought supernatural breakthrough in our city. We launched our own Healing Prayer Centre in 2006.

At the end of one of our conferences we had a 'fire tunnel' – a way of blessing a lot of people in a short time with joy, laughter and the baptism of fire from the Holy Spirit. So as the band and I continued to celebrate passionately we assembled our prayer team in two rows, much as guests would see off a bride and groom at the end of a wedding feast.

From the platform I had a perfect view of the orderly chaos that ensued as people entered the tunnel and began to shake, laugh and get overwhelmed by Holy Spirit. Some were unable to walk after a few steps and fell to the ground, then needed to be gently dragged aside to make room for those who followed behind. It was glorious to see something we had previously experienced in other nations happening in our own service. We ended up with a pile of bodies at the exit of the tunnel, all experiencing a personal touch from God.

It reminded me of some of the stories of revival when people were mightily touched by a sovereign move of God, swooning with what felt like electricity pulsing through their bodies. A friend of mine sidled up and whispered in my ear, 'You can stop praying that prayer now. God is doing here what he did in Toronto!' As we dug in for a move of God, he met us with rivers of living water flowing in and through his people.

A few years later we were hosting another conference called 'Encounter Heaven.' The times of worship went very deep, from holy ground moments to exuberant celebration where the whole room ended up in spontaneous dance which went on for about an hour. I've never seen anything like it in church before!

And then something really unusual happened. Perhaps it

was the lights we had on the stage, but someone from the pub up the road thought the church was on fire. While the joyful dancing was going on in the sanctuary, the fire brigade pulled up in an engine to find out what was burning. It was just the hearts of his passionate people!

I believe the wells we dug in those years led to an 'outpouring in our city, the like of which we had not previously experienced. While God was moving in Lakeland, Florida in 2008 we began to host weekly meetings that filled our building with over three hundred people. Three weeks later we moved to Central Hall and held gatherings of around six to seven hundred people every Monday night for months!

Every time we met the worship was intense, and people were healed, inspired and strengthened. It was a very precious season of my life and I honour our amazing team for being such gracious hosts. I believe the spiritual water table in our city rose over those special months.

In April of 2009 Randy Clark, Bill Johnson and Leif Hetland came to deliver a Global Awakening School of Healing and Impartation (now called Kingdom Foundations). The place was filled to capacity and we had over one hundred leaders from twenty European nations there. It was a highlight of my life to host the event and lead some intense times of worship in this building, itself an historic well of revival where the likes of George Geoffrey, Smith Wigglesworth and Billy Graham have preached and ministered.

Around the building were queues of people waiting to get in, as they did so many years previously. These modern-day revivalists, who have impacted many nations in the world, delivered timely messages of supernatural release and revelation in our own city. During this powerful outpouring of Holy Spirit, people committed themselves to the Lord's purposes on their lives and there were many significant, documented healings. I still get testimonies years later! Afterwards people were inspired to go 'treasure hunting' (a type of prophetic evangelism) on our streets and there was an increase in healing in our own healing services and healing rooms.

When we praise we are ploughing the ground ready for planting. We prepare for the next harvest in the cycle of sowing and reaping in God's kingdom. When we worship we dig down to the streams of living water to release them to flow, from our innermost being, or corporately.

God's strategies are revealed and our battle changes situations in ways we may not understand fully. In faith we obey his instruction and guidance. If we engage with him and his purposes intentionally, a neighbourhood, city, a region, or even a nation can be transformed!

10

'ON EARTH AS IT IS IN HEAVEN'

His presence in the atmosphere

When I was a child at St Mark's middle school, we still prayed the old version of the Lord's Prayer in assembly: 'Our Father who art in heaven, hallowed be thy name, thy kingdom come, thy will be done on earth as it is in heaven...' I used to think that heaven was a place that is far away and in the future, with God sitting on a distant cloud!

The Greek word ouranos means the sky and, by extension, heaven or the dwelling place of God. The same word is sometimes translated 'air,' e.g. the birds of the air (Matthew 6:26). So really we can pray, 'My Father, you are right here in front of me, in the air I breathe and all around me. Holy and wonderful is your Name...'

Thankfully the Lord's Prayer doesn't start with 'O God, these are my problems here on earth!' When we focus on the presence the problems fall into perspective. So we turn our face to the Face (Hebrew: panim), and pray 'Father...'

The Bible is full of interactions between God and us via the air...

... where his voice speaks to us:

...and behold, a voice from heaven said, 'This is my beloved Son, with whom I am well pleased.' (Matthew 3:17 ESV)

... or manifestations come from:

And suddenly there came from heaven a sound like a mighty rushing wind, and it filled the entire house where they were sitting. (Acts 2:2 ESV)

... where we look up to:

Then he ordered the crowds to sit down on the grass, and taking the five loaves and the two fish, he looked up to heaven and said a blessing. Then he broke the loaves and gave them to the disciples, and the disciples gave them to the crowds. (Matthew 14:19 ESV)

... where the Holy Spirit comes down from:

And John bore witness: 'I saw the Spirit descend from heaven like a dove, and it remained on him.' (John 1:32 ESV)

... where Jesus ascends to:

While he blessed them, he parted from them and was carried up into heaven. (Luke 24:51 ESV)

... where things come down from:

[Peter] saw the heavens opened and something like a great sheet descending, being let down by its four corners upon the earth. (Acts 10:11 ESV)

Heaven and earth may be separate realms, but the Bible shows they interact with each other in our realm; we call it space and time.

So, what is heaven? It's the place where God lives.

Where is heaven? It's in the atmosphere from the air around our heads to beyond the stars.

When is heaven? It's here and now!

Mission Earth

Our mission, should we decide to accept it, is to bring heaven to earth: the bounty, the fullness, the power, the love, the kindness, the grace, the forgiveness. Everything that belongs to heaven belongs to us, so we can bring it to wherever we are.

Jesus said the kingdom of heaven is near! He said, 'change the way you think because the kingdom of heaven is at hand' – right there on the end of his arm (Matthew 4:17)! He wasn't joking when he prayed, 'on earth as it is in heaven.' Jesus was able to live in and from the kingdom, and we need to learn to live like that.

Often Jesus exercised his power in personal dealings with people. Heidi Baker says, 'love looks like something' – it's not just words. It's practical, powerful and kind; it's caring and it breaks chains. She also says 'stop for the one,' just like Jesus did. So our model is to stop for the one in front of us, and freely give away what we have, whether love, time, wisdom, healing or finance.

Jesus' power exercised in humility and love caused people to seek him. This in itself is spectacular. But God does what he pleases, and sometimes chooses to do things with Hollywood special effects! Such glorious manifestations of his presence also cause people to seek him.

The wind and fire of Pentecost (Acts 2) resulted in a multi-lingual outpouring of praise. At nine in the morning the square outside the building where the wind blew was full of people drawn by the unusual sound. Peter explained to the curious assembly what was happening and told them about Jesus, so three thousand people became Christians that day and the church was born. Psalm 29 describes the thundering voice of the Lord shaking the desert and splintering the mighty cedar trees: God can move powerfully as well as intimately. Earthquakes can follow prayer meetings (Acts 4:23-29) and prison escapes and multiple salvations accompany praise services (Acts 16) – all signs that make people wonder.

These signs and wonders should be following us everywhere we go and pointing to the magnificent Saviour, Jesus!

It does appear that God inhabits public declarations of spontaneous praise and adoration with spectacular results. They cause people to seek him and provide us with an opportunity to tell them about him. Perhaps we should take praise out into the streets and see what God does!

His presence in music

By now I hope you grasped the concept that God inhabits

prophetic singing and music, which causes people to seek him: *He put a new song in my mouth, a hymn of praise to our God. Many will see and fear and put their trust in the LORD.* (Psalm 40:3 NIV)

Words and music work together as the lyrics gain access to our minds and the music accesses our emotions to prepare our hearts to receive the words. When words are encased in a stream of music they can deeply influence our thoughts and actions. So songs can have a very powerful effect on us which, if our heart allows, can influence our sense of right and wrong and our will to act.

We are warned in scripture that there is life and death in the tongue (Proverbs 18:21, James 3). We are also exhorted to understand what is good and what is evil (Hebrews 5) and to have our senses trained. We should be discerning so that when something comes on television or radio that doesn't resonate with our spirit, we change the channel or turn it off.

Listen to the right voice. In war it's more important to destroy the morale of the troops, than the troops themselves. So pay attention to whatever is good, noble, etc. When the Holy Spirit speaks, listen! Jesus loves what's right and he hates all evil.

Songs can have a damaging effect or do enormous good. A musician full of the Holy Spirit will release the Spirit of God in a place when they play. A musician whose motives are of a darker persuasion will release something altogether different. We don't avoid using swords just because the enemy uses them. War is war and weapons are required. Which side we are on determines whether we use those weapons for good or evil.

David understood the relationship between praise and warfare:

Praise the LORD. Sing to the LORD a new song, his praise in the assembly of the saints. Let Israel rejoice in their Maker; let the people of Zion be glad in their King. Let them praise his name with dancing and make music to him with tambourine (drum) and harp. For the LORD takes delight in his people; he crowns the humble with salvation. Let the saints rejoice in this honour and sing for joy on their beds. May the praise of God be in their mouths and a double-edged sword in their hands, to inflict vengeance on the nations and punishment on the peoples, to bind their kings with fetters, their nobles with shackles of iron, to carry out the sentence written against them. This is the glory of all his saints. Praise the LORD. (Psalm 149 NIV)

That's a pretty aggressive song, inflicting vengeance and punishment, chaining up the enemy and so on. Yet it was a praise song and I can imagine it had quite a lot of drums in it!

For many years our team has taken care to choose a fitting style of instrumentation and music to accompany a prophetic song or word. The music must convey the sense of the words. God summons us into his battle with him and warfare requires warfare music. When the God of angel armies (2 Kings 6:17) goes to war, soft serenades are inappropriate. We do not pronounce death to the enemy with ballads!

Strike the drum

There has been an unfortunate translation of the Hebrew word toph. Psalm 81 says, 'begin the music, strike the timbrel or tambourine.' Imagine for a moment the Levite priests in a mighty gathering of praise. Trumpets and rams' horns blast, unified voices shout loudly and our percussionist slaps a round thing with jingles on it.... no, no, no!

The toph was a frame drum with a goatskin stretched over it. It was made in different sizes, some of which were very portable like Miriam's drum (Exodus 15:20). Rattling metal things were not attached to drums in those days! Toph is onomatopoeic and when that instrument was thumped it made a deep loud sound. TOPH! BOOM!

So begin the music, strike the drum – whatever you have, the bigger the better! Because when you strike a drum you shift air, it is simple physics. So when Christian drummers strike their drums they shift the air and who is the prince and power of the air (Ephesians 2:2)? Yes, he who shall not be named. So every time we play our instruments and raise our voices we shake the atmosphere. In that spiritual realm where God lives, heaven is released and transformation begins.

When someone says drums are of the devil, they have not understood the Bible. There are seventeen references to actual drums (not tambourines) in scripture. Drums are very important in making music, especially warfare music. I believe we are recapturing the sound of warfare in our high praise and drums are part of this.

The voice of God thunders majestically and with excellence (Job 37:5) and there is definitely a time and a place to thunder with our drums. We echo that sound, show forth our musical excellence, praise him and intercede with the sound of warfare. (And by the way, there are no pipe organs in the Bible, but we do have those in some churches, don't we!)

In his presence
You make known to me the path of life; in your presence there is fullness of joy. (Psalm 16:11 ESV)

At a conference a few years ago, where we were leading worship, the music and prophetic songs were once again a launch pad for heaven to invade earth. The tangible presence of God filled Central Hall in Southampton, and I had a strong sense of God wanting to bring different kinds of healing, especially for emotional and psychological disorders.

The joy of the Lord really is our strength and I felt there was a breakthrough that night for people from fear, anxiety and depression. I also knew joy was about to be released in the room: sometimes I can just feel these things bubbling up in my spirit and pockets of laughter were breaking out around the room.

During the worship I went after healing by calling out a number of conditions I felt the Lord had put on my heart and then inviting people to respond and receive sovereignly from

God. I could see people encountering the Holy Spirit around the room. The band continued to play and we just made space for heaven to come to earth and touch people's lives.

A very good friend of mine, Martin, has been used by God on a number of occasions to release joy to others. I could hear him laughing up on the top balcony and encouraged him to come down and give away what he was receiving but he was unable to walk, incapacitated by joyful hilarity. That kind of joy is very infectious and it quickly spread as people trying to help him down the steps came under the influence themselves!

After some time and much laughter we eventually got Martin to a chair near the stage. Though he was clearly incapable of laying hands on people, we got a couple of friends to help and as people came forward for a 'joy blessing' they either laid hands on him or someone placed Martin's hand on them. It was wonderful to see the lightness break out in the room!

Many lives were deeply touched that night. The same people who were on their knees with tears streaming down their cheeks were a little later laughing and rolling around the floor. I love the fact that something wonderful always happens when we make room to encounter the King of Glory. It's amazing and I know that God is doing far more than we can see with our eyes.

Recently I heard a remarkable testimony from someone, now a close friend, whose life was profoundly changed that evening. This is Emma's story:

I struggled with depression for most of my teenage years and into my mid-twenties, to the point that friends who know me well suggested I should be on medication. The struggle became a little easier when I was born again, but the dark cloud of sadness didn't lift. I didn't want to be on medication, so I battled on, holding out for God to heal me.

One evening at a prophetic conference, during the worship time, Alun Leppitt was leading worship and calling out what God was doing – including healing depression. As soon as he said the word depression I flew backwards two or three seats and landed on the floor. I knew something had happened and then I realised I was healed of depression in an instant! The old feeling of heaviness and sadness had just gone.

Since that night I have not struggled with depression and I walk in ever-increasing levels of joy. There are times when the enemy tries to take a shot at me, but he can't get me down for long because of this lasting breakthrough that happened in an instant. Joy is a huge part of who I am now – it's part of my identity. 'In all my circumstances my joy knows no bounds.' (Emma West)

Emma is now one of the most joyful people I know and I'm so thankful to God for breaking this condition from her life and bring a permanent transformation for her. Yay God!

Born for battle

Referring to King David's fall from grace in 2 Samuel 11 when he stayed at home from the battle in Jerusalem, Bill Johnson says:

'David lost the battle with his eyes, which opened the door for him to lose the battle with his heart, all because he wasn't in the battle he was born for.'

During the spring time when kings go out to war, this king stayed at home and got mightily distracted by a bathing beauty, who coincidently was called Bathsheba. David was born for conquest and triumph, to establish Israel's victory in other nations and bring about a lasting peace for future generations. But away from the battlefield his eyes wandered, he lost his focus, which led to a series of moral failures!

Each one of us is born for places of victory, for triumphs and breakthroughs and to significantly influence those around us. When we are removed from or deliberately turn away from the battle we've been assigned to, we then face a battle we're not equipped for.

In varying measure we have been trained, equipped and prepared. We've studied the Bible, listened to hundreds of sermons, attended conferences, received 'downloads' of wisdom and revelation, and had hands laid on us to receive grace gifts. So through the indwelling Holy Spirit's anointing, at any given moment we are ready to release that which is in us and on us. We are ready to bring heaven to earth and to bring about a righteous influence.

When we lose track of this we become subject to what we are not ready for. Distracted, confused, isolated, bored, perhaps weighed down and depressed, we can become lost. So we need to find our place and be all that we can be, covered by all who God is.

Divine impact of praise and worship

Let's look possibly the best demonstration of the impact of praise and worship in the context of warfare. 2 Chronicles 20 describes how King Jehoshaphat was under mortal threat from a vast invading army. As a wise king he turned his attention to the Lord and then immediately called the nation together to fast and seek God.

How many times when we face challenges, do we bring forth opinions and feelings instead of waiting on the Lord and listening to the wise counsel that comes from him? We won't find the answer in the problem, but we will find it in his presence.

Jehoshaphat prayed before the assembly, declaring God's power and greatness. He recalled historic victories, inviting God to do the same again. Men, women and children all gathered to wait on God. Then a prophet addressed the assembly with the word of the Lord. They could have dismissed his words but they listened and acted: take heed of your prophets and you will prosper.

And the Spirit of the Lord came upon Jahaziel…a Levite of the sons of Asaph, in the midst of the assembly. And he said, 'Listen, all Judah and inhabitants of Jerusalem and King Jehoshaphat: Thus says the Lord to you, "Do not be afraid and do not be dismayed at this great horde, for the battle is not yours but God's. Tomorrow go down against them. Behold, they will come up by the ascent of Ziz. You will find them at the end of the valley, east of the wilderness of Jeruel."' (2 Chronicles 20:14-16 ESV)

Under the influence of the Spirit, Jahaziel declared that the people were not to fear. His words bring courage today as they did all those years ago – the battle is not yours, it is God's!

Stand firm, then. This is the battle position that God is calling the church to take. If you're in the right place, stay there; if you're not, find out where you should be and get there, because when you find your right place you will win battles. 'Stand firm, and after having done everything, stand' (Ephesians 6).

When the strategy for victory was revealed, peace came to the king and his people and they bowed down together. Then the Levites stood and praised the Lord. The divine strategy for winning the battle was loud worship in the face of the enemy.

Don't be afraid

They went out with the musicians and the singers at the front of the army. They were in the vanguard – a very important spiritual principle. When David full of the Holy Spirit played his harp he brought deliverance to a demonised King Saul. Judah went out giving praise to the Lord and the enemy was thrown into confusion; God used him to set ambushes.

After consulting the people, Jehoshaphat appointed men to sing to the Lord and to praise him for the splendour of his holiness as they went out at the head of the army, saying: 'Give thanks to the Lord, for his love endures forever.' As they began to sing and praise, the Lord set ambushes against the men of Ammon and Moab and Mount Seir who were invading Judah, and they were defeated. (2 Chronicles 20:21-22 NIV)

Let God arise and let his enemies be scattered! He is a God of war, and is calling forth a militant sound that has been missing in the church. Here is another prophetic picture:

And the Lord will cause his majestic voice to be heard and the descending blow of his arm to be seen, in furious anger and a flame of devouring fire, with a cloudburst and storm and hailstones. The Assyrians will be terror-stricken at the voice of the Lord, when he strikes with his rod. And every stroke of the appointed staff that the Lord lays on them will be to the sound of tambourines (drums) and lyres. Battling with brandished arm, he will fight with them. (Isaiah 30:30-32, ESV)

This 'appointed staff' is also translated as God's 'punishing rod.' The Lord says he's going to use his big stick to bash the living daylights out of the enemy! And it will happen as we strike the drum and play the guitars – as *we* play our part *he* will win the battle.

Our posture, attitude and actions affect the atmosphere and release the angelic realm to bring victory. What we do with our instruments and our bodies in obedient response to the Lord is key – often we witness an outpouring of Holy Spirit or a breakout of healing in the room after we have released prophetic declarations and songs. As we play spontaneously under the unction of Holy Spirit, darkness flees.

Know your enemy
In order to fight our enemy, it's important to know at least a little bit about him. My focus is on Jesus, so I don't give Satan any glory. I pay as little attention as possible to him, I silence his lies in my ears and I don't answer his calls!

There is scriptural evidence of three archangels in the beginning: Michael the warrior (Revelation 12:7), Gabriel the messenger (Luke 1:26-28), and Lucifer the worship leader (based on Job 37:47 where the morning stars sang at creation and his title of 'morning star' in Isaiah 14:12).

The name Lucifer is the King James rendering of the Hebrew helel or heylel found only in Isaiah 14:2 which means 'shining one' or morning star. The Latin Vulgate translates this word as 'Lucifer', meaning the morning star or 'light-bringer.' It has the word hallal (praise) at its root.

The problem was that Lucifer wanted the worship for himself and so was cast out of heaven (Isaiah 14:12-15, Ezekiel

28:12-19) with a third of the angels (Revelation 12:4), likely those serving under him to bring worship to God. As one who led worship, he knows only too well the power of music and creativity, but he wants them used for his own glory and to war against God.

However, if heaven has lost its singers, musicians and creative beings, then we on the earth have the awesome privilege of surrounding God's throne with offerings of worship. Dave Markee makes this point in his excellent book, *The Lost Glory*, and the last twenty years I have seen God restoring the arts, creative freedom, prophecy, worship and musical excellence in the church.

The filling of the airwaves
Whether or not we are persuaded by this account of Satan's origins, there is little doubt that he has been given the rule over the earth and desires worship for himself:

Again, the devil took him to a very high mountain and showed him all the kingdoms of the world and their glory. And he said to him, 'All these I will give you, if you will fall down and worship me.' Then Jesus said to him, 'Be gone, Satan! For it is written, "You shall worship the Lord your God and him only shall you serve."' Then the devil left him, and behold, angels came and were ministering to him. (Matthew 4:8-11 ESV)

Also, the enemy wars against those who will not give him worship:

For we do not wrestle against flesh and blood, but against the rulers, against the authorities, against the cosmic powers over this present darkness, against the spiritual forces of evil in the heavenly places. (Ephesians 6:12 ESV)

Because of this we're advised to wear our spiritual armour and stand firm. The war is fought especially through the creative arts because God is a creator and designed creativity to communicate truth.

For what can be known about God is plain to them, because God has shown it to them. For his invisible attributes, namely, his eternal power and divine nature, have been clearly perceived, ever since the creation of the world, in the things that have been made. So they are without excuse. (Romans 1:19-20 ESV)

Even if we're not taught we can understand things about the maker from what has been made. All the creative arts have power to influence our thoughts and our emotions. Jesus taught using stories, metaphors and pictures to make his teaching more vivid and memorable. He described the kingdom of God as a mustard seed or treasure hidden in a field, for example.

In our celebrity-worshipping culture, those who practice creative arts (singers, musicians, artists, actors) are worshiped and rewarded highly. We join their fan clubs, we buy their products, we follow their lives in the media, we aspire to talk like them and even to look like them. We have given them tremendous power over us.

And what message are we getting through their art? It's not the Ten Commandments or the message of Jesus! Then who is shaping our thoughts, feelings and sense of right and wrong through this powerful means of communication? It is the 'father of lies.'

Jesus had this to say about him:

He was a murderer from the beginning, not holding to the truth, for there is no truth in him. When he lies, he speaks his native language, for he is a liar and the father of lies. (John 8:44 NIV)

The enemy can't change the truth but tries to make us disbelieve it. And if we fall for that, our unbelief can prevent us from receiving God's love and the power of heaven, because unbelief insulates us from God's power (Mark 6:5).

The identity crisis
Disappointments, hurts, relational breakdown, church politics, and spiritual abuse all challenge our faith. Many things in life are not ordained by God, but used by the enemy to cause us

to stop really believing. Yet one of the most powerful things on the planet is a believing believer! The father of lies wants to stop us from really 'getting' the truth about God, so we won't take territory from him. In some churches people are busy doing that work for him, with slander, criticism, jealousy, competition, unkindness, selfish behaviour and so on. Disunity, backbiting and unbelief all build the wrong kingdom.

Unless we see each other as God sees us, then we will not have victory. We are called to be one in spirit and purpose, just as Jesus and God are one (Philippians 2:2). Jesus is coming for a beautiful, spotless bride, not a bruised girl in a torn, dirty dress, so let us celebrate what we agree on rather than what separates us. The kingdom of heaven will be built on relationships, which are far more important than correctness on an issue.

The Protestant church has been founded on protesting, and history has many sad examples of churches separating over doctrinal issues. God wants his children to get along, and to gather around spiritual mothers and fathers in relationship. Everyone in a family should be able to sit around a table and share a meal regardless of differences of opinion.

Recently God gave me a picture of the Levites carrying the glowing Ark of the Covenant on poles between their shoulders. For me the poles represented strong and sturdy relationships that are able to carry the weight of glory. The stronger our relationships, the greater the glory of God can be over our lives. We need to be real with people and walk shoulder to shoulder with them in love.

Every word spoken over our lives from God will be contested by the enemy before very long. When our heavenly purpose becomes known in the enemy camp, we may experience opposition and an undermining of that call.

But the Lord holds our destiny. In the story of Jehoshaphat, the people spent three days collecting the spoils of battle, and we too will win valuable things when we fight for them.

The sword strapped to King David's waist that he used

in war, was the sword of Goliath (1 Samuel 21:9). The very weapon Goliath wanted to kill him with, became the sword David used in his future battles. So it is with us. When we win a battle it will give us weapons to bring victory for others. It's not enough to be set free; we are called to become 'freedom fighters' of the kingdom.

The fight for hearts and minds

Here are four ways we can wage war in the arena of music and the creative arts:

1. Let us strengthen our defences by being wise about the music we listen to, the TV programmes or films we watch, the books or magazines we read and the stuff we view on the internet. They will influence our beliefs and imprint on our thought life. Take every thought captive.

2. Let us go on the offensive by enjoying music, films and books that are beautiful containers of truth, and supporting creative people who make these quality materials so that they may prosper. Let us also be creators ourselves.

3. Let us wholeheartedly worship God, offering ourselves as living sacrifices. Jesus is seated at the right hand of the Father (Romans 8:34), so if we are joined to him, when we look over our left shoulder we will see our heavenly Father! That gives us great courage and boldness.

4. Let us fill the airwaves around our heads with 'psalms, hymns and spiritual songs' so that God inhabits that space rather than the enemy. The spacious and peaceful place around us will then draw people to seek him.

God is searching the earth for those that truly love him (John 4:23) and for those in whom he can show himself strong (2 Chronicles 16:19). He asks us to involve ourselves in his plans.

God's battle plan for the last days

The famous vision of the valley of dry bones (Ezekiel 37:1-14) tells us that God is in the business of breathing life into dried out, separated people, and marshalling them as a huge army to retake possession of their territory. The key of David refers to possessing legitimate, God given authority. God

wants to raise up his people with keys of authority and so affect our spheres of influence.

Then he said to me, 'Prophesy to the breath; prophesy son of man, and say to it, "This is what the Sovereign Lord says: Come from the four winds, O breath, and breathe into these slain, that they may live."' So I prophesied as he commanded me, and breath entered them; they came to life and stood up on their feet – a vast army. (Ezekiel 37:9-10 NIV)

It wasn't a church God breathed life into, it was an army. An army battles for territory, and I believe it's time to win back all that the enemy has stolen.

1. To pour out his Spirit

As God's people are re-established into their territory, God's Spirit pours out upon them, bringing new gifts with accompanying signs and wonders. This causes people to call out to God to be saved. This was Peter's interpretation of the events at Pentecost as prophesied by Joel

In the last days, God says, I will pour out my Spirit on all people. Your sons and daughters will prophesy, your young men will see visions, your old men will dream dreams. Even on my servants, both men and women, I will pour out my Spirit in those days, and they will prophesy. I will show wonders in the heaven above and signs on the earth below, blood and fire and billows of smoke. The sun will be turned to darkness and the moon to blood before the coming of the great and glorious day of the Lord. And everyone who calls on the name of the Lord will be saved. (Acts 2:17-21 NIV)

In the last few decades, incredible revivals have been occurring in many different parts of the world among people who have been seeking him. The result is salvations and baptisms, physical and emotional healing, deliverance and freedom, calls to the mission field, and society-changing transformation. Even barren fields become abundantly fruitful, as God hears from heaven and works through his people.

2. To establish his kingdom

When God pours out his Spirit on people, they can begin the work of establishing his kingdom on earth as it is in heaven. Jesus saw this as his purpose (Luke 4:18-19).

The Spirit of the Sovereign LORD is on me, because the LORD has anointed me to preach good news to the poor. He has sent me to bind up the broken-hearted, to proclaim freedom for the captives and release from darkness for the prisoners, to proclaim the year of the LORD's favour and the day of vengeance of our God, to comfort all who mourn, and provide for those who grieve in Zion – to bestow on them a crown of beauty instead of ashes, the oil of gladness instead of mourning, and a garment of praise instead of a spirit of despair. They will be called oaks of righteousness, a planting of the LORD for the display of his splendour. They will rebuild the ancient ruins and restore the places long devastated; they will renew the ruined cities that have been devastated for generations. (Isaiah 61:1-4 NIV)

For far too long the church has kept the work of the Spirit within its four walls. What Jesus spoke out in the synagogue is a mandate for all our lives; it is the call over the church.

The Spirit of the Sovereign Lord is upon us, so we will bind up broken hearts, we will release the captives, we will open blind eyes, we will bring joy and gladness, we will see our cities touched and changed, all in the name of Jesus! Let us go with him into the world, transforming it by love.

3. To restore a tent

When God's people commit themselves to him and his cause and *'let justice roll on like a river, righteousness like a never-failing stream'* (Amos 5:24), his presence is restored.

'After this I will return and rebuild David's fallen tent. Its ruins I will rebuild, and I will restore it, that the remnant of men may

seek the Lord, and all the Gentiles who bear my name,' says the Lord, who does these things. (Acts 15:16-17 NIV)

The time for this is coming and we must make preparation, particularly by our prophetic songs. God inhabits them and displaces the enemy in the airwaves. We need to be trained by God in warfare music to take territory back from the enemy.

David clearly understood this: *'Praise be to the LORD my Rock, who trains my hands for war, my fingers for battle'* (Psalm 144:1 NIV). I believe the restoration of his tabernacle causes people to seek God and thus, in Reinhard Bonnke's words, *'we are to plunder hell to populate heaven.'*

11

THIS THANKFUL HEART

THE POWER OF GRATITUDE

The one who offers thanksgiving as his sacrifice glorifies me.
(Psalm 50:23 ESV)

Gratitude is the password into the presence of God. Giving thanks to God in all things, even unseen blessings, is how we draw near to him. Psalm 100 lays out a symbolic approach into the throne-room of God:

Make a joyful noise to the Lord, all the earth! Serve the Lord with gladness! Come into his presence with singing! Know that the Lord, he is God! It is he who made us, and we are his; we are his people, and the sheep of his pasture. Enter his gates with thanksgiving, and his courts with praise! Give thanks to him; bless his name! For the Lord is good; his steadfast love endures forever, and his faithfulness to all generations. (Psalm 100 ESV)

We enter his gates with thanksgiving and come into his courts with praise. We come into his presence with singing, or as the Message translation says, 'Sing yourself into his presence!'

Charles Spurgeon eloquently said of Psalm 100:

'Let us sing the Old Hundredth' is one of the every-day expressions of the Christian church, and will be so while men, exist whose hearts are loyal to the Great King. Nothing can be more sublime this side heaven than the singing of this noble psalm by a vast congregation.

The invitation to worship here given is not a melancholy one, as though adoration were a funeral solemnity, but a cheery gladsome exhortation, as though we were bidden to a marriage feast. Come before his presence with singing. We ought in worship to realise the presence of God, and by an effort of the mind to approach him...

The measured, harmonious, hearty utterance of praise by a congregation of really devout persons is not merely decorous but delightful, and is a fit anticipation of the worship of heaven, where praise has absorbed prayer, and become the sole mode of adoration.' (The Treasury of David – Charles H Spurgeon)

The password into the presence, the 'Access All Areas' backstage pass, is joyfully shouting our gratitude and glad praises, coming ever deeper into his goodness and mercy.

'...make a sanctuary for me, and I will dwell among them.' (Exodus 25:8 NIV)

The Lord clearly planned this for his people to draw close to him in the wilderness and in the Promised Land. I believe this blueprint still applies today as he desires to dwell among his people in the beauty of a 'sanctuary.'

The tabernacle of Moses

The intricate design for the tabernacle was laid out by God face to face with Moses (Exodus chapters 25-28). It was not a permanent structure, because when the pillar of fire moved so did the people and the tabernacle. It had a traditional shape with a 75 by 150 foot outer court and a 15 by 45 foot structure in the back (Exodus 27:9-19). The walls were linen curtains attached by bronze hooks to a series of pillars supported by bronze sockets. The priests placed the tabernacle so that the gate, about 30 feet wide, always faced east.

The actual tent sat in the back of the courtyard (Exodus 26). The sides and back were gold-covered wooden acacia boards, about 28 inches wide and 15 feet high. Each board had two interlocking tenons, which fitted into silver sockets.

Gold rings held five bars that ran the length of the boards, holding them tight. The east side was comprised of five pillars covered with a screen.

The tent was divided into two rooms: the Holy Place, where the table of showbread, the golden lamp stand, and the altar of incense sat; and the Holy of Holies, where the Ark of the Covenant resided. This sacred room was a 15-foot cube separated from the Holy Place by a thick curtain. The curtain was embroidered with cherubim and hung from four gold-covered acacia posts by gold clasps. This veil or screen was made of fine linen and blue, purple and scarlet yarn.

This purpose of this curtain was to shield sinful man from the holy presence of Almighty God, and only the high priest entered this sacred dwelling once a year on the Day of Atonement.

However, Jesus' sacrificial death on the cross changed that. When he died, the curtain in the Jerusalem temple was torn in half, from the top to the bottom, a supernatural feat performed by the hand of God. It gave free access to the presence of the Father for all the sons of God, for all time! The age of animal offerings was over as the ultimate offering had been sacrificed.

Therefore, brothers, since we have confidence to enter the Most Holy Place by the blood of Jesus, by a new and living way opened for us through the curtain, that is, his body … let us draw near to God with a sincere heart in full assurance of faith. (Hebrews 10:19-22 ESV)

The fear of the Lord

The awesome sacrifice of Jesus, the Great High Priest, means we have access for all times into the throne-room (Hebrews 6:19-20). Yet we must not be complacent about the great privilege we have to host the holy presence of God.

The fear of the Lord is the beginning of wisdom, and we need wisdom as we enter his courts. So let us not come casually into his holy presence, but enter intentionally and with thanksgiving. We approach with reverent devotion because he alone is truly worthy to receive all our honour and all our praise! And let the incense of our hearts, minds and bodies arise day and night.

The intricate formalities for worship in the Mosaic temple that were simplified and continued in David's tent can still be an example for us in these New Covenant days, with foundational truths for God's people to come into an intimate relationship with him.

Psalm 100 calls us to enter his presence with thanksgiving and praise. Each of us is to lay down our lives on the altar of sacrifice by giving God our best, our first fruits. God invites each one of us to draw even closer, to linger even longer in his beautiful presence, so we can know and be known.

Transformation happens here. He removes the dross to refine his treasure. As we wait on the Lord we gain renewed strength; our bodies are energised, our emotional batteries are recharged, and our spirits soar like eagles (Isaiah 40:31). We receive inspired thoughts and God reveals his purposes for us. In this place of divine exchange, what is designed for God's glory ends up blessing us!

The abundance of the heart

A good man out of the good treasure of his heart brings forth good; and an evil man out of the evil treasure of his heart brings forth evil. For out of the abundance of the heart his mouth speaks. (Luke 6:45 ESV)

We need to watch what we say. Remember, faith comes by hearing and we hear what we ourselves say, whether it is about bad stuff happening or trusting God's word and promise. Scepticism insulates us from the miraculous power of God, as Jesus' neighbours found out in the synagogue in Nazareth (Mark 6:1-6). Jesus was amazed at their unbelief and could work no miracles there.

What comes out of our mouths should be tempered by grace and bring the positivity and wisdom of the kingdom of

God to every situation. This is especially true when we talk about people. After creating us in his image God, declared that we were very good! So speak positively of yourself and each other and rejoice always – it's a powerful way to change the atmosphere.

We can express our gratitude to God for what he has done, whether or not we feel spiritual and full of faith. It is important to remember what he has done this day, this week, this month, this year, or at significant points in our life and thank him for protecting us from circumstances that may have harmed us.

God is good all the time and has good things for us and good things for us to do. Giving thanks is like a runway to the supply plane of heaven, preparing the way for God to show us his nature.

Activating the will

Sometimes we just need to choose to activate our will over life's circumstances. David wrote::

I will give thanks to the Lord with my whole heart; I will recount all of your wonderful deeds. I will be glad and exult in you; I will sing praise to your name, O Most High. (Psalm 9:1-2 ESV)

Sometimes the psalmist starts in a low place but then says, 'I will remember,' 'I will trust in your unfailing love,' 'I will proclaim,' 'I will not fear,' 'I will give thanks,' 'I will sing,' 'I will be glad.' He continues on, powerfully declaring God's nature in all circumstances. We can make the decision and just do it, remembering God's goodness.

Prime the pump

When my father was a child in South Wales, he regularly went to the village well to get water for the family. If he was the first to arrive in the morning, he would 'prime the pump' to bring the water to the surface pipe after gravity had caused it to fall back to the water table overnight. He had to pump hard at first, but once the water was flowing, it was easy for him and everyone else to draw their water.

Thanksgiving will prime the pump of your heart. Let the living water bubble up inside you. Whatever kind of day we have had, however we feel, we can thank God for who he is and what he has done. It doesn't take long before the fountain of life can come bursting forth. Remembering what God has already done can also bring us courage to persevere, pressing in for more.

Remember who you are

Before David fought Goliath he had an audience with King Saul and recounted how he protected his father's herds from the bears and the lion (1 Samuel 17). As he recalled how God preserved him, his faith and courage arose.

Out on the battlefield the army of Israel may have looked the part clothed in armour, but they lacked the courage to face the Philistine champion. But David knew the anointing on his life for godly purpose and he knew his God, so he ran straight at the large obstacle before him.

David picked up five stones in the brook, not because he distrusted his aim, but because he knew that Goliath had four brothers. He confidently planned ahead for the event of the brothers marching onto the battlefield themselves.

Remember what the Lord has done, and his promise to be with us always. He gives us victory and he has overcome the world! So we take the ground before us and then move forward.

The past is past

The enemy tries to point at your failures and make them your future, robbing you of your provision. But God says all that is forgiven and forgotten; the past is past. Our mistakes are part of our schooling, and failures are not 'disqualifiers' in the kingdom. We are not who our circumstances say we are; we are who God says we are. We were once sinners but have been saved by grace and now we are the righteousness of God.

Give thanks always:

...giving thanks always and for everything to God the Father in the name of our Lord Jesus Christ. (Ephesians 5:20 ESV)

Give thanks in everything:

...give thanks in all circumstances; for this is the will of God in Christ Jesus for you. (1 Thessalonians 5:18 ESV)

And rejoice!

Rejoice in the Lord always; again I will say, rejoice. Let your reasonableness be known to everyone. The Lord is at hand; do not be anxious about anything, but in everything by prayer and supplication with thanksgiving let your requests be made known to God. And the peace of God, which surpasses all understanding, will guard your hearts and your minds in Christ Jesus. (Philippians 4:4-7 ESV)

Our joy is in him, not in our circumstances, because he is the same yesterday, today and forever. When we celebrate the outcome before it has happened, then we are preparing for the breakthrough he promises. So we give God thanks for what he has done, for who he is, and for what he will do.

One in ten

On the way to Jerusalem he was passing along between Samaria and Galilee. And as he entered a village, he was met by ten lepers, who stood at a distance and lifted up their voices, saying, 'Jesus, Master, have mercy on us.' When he saw them he said to them, 'Go and show yourselves to the priests.' And as they went they were cleansed. Then one of them, when he saw that he was healed, turned back, praising God with a loud voice; and he fell on his face at Jesus' feet, giving him thanks. Now he was a Samaritan. Then Jesus answered, 'Were not ten cleansed? Where are the nine? Was no one found to return and give praise to God except this foreigner?' And he said to him, 'Rise and go your way; your faith has made you well [has saved you].' (Luke 17:11-19 ESV)

Only one leper came back shouting God's praises and fell at Jesus' feet to give thanks for his miracle. Ten lepers were cleansed, but only the foreigner came back and received something the others didn't: he was made whole! Thanksgiving was the tipping point for this blessing, bringing deep wholeness and even salvation.

The nine other ex-lepers must have been delighted to return to their family and community, but they inadvertently missed out on something more that came through thanksgiving. We receive more when we acknowledge what the Lord has done for us, however big or small. The Samaritan was an outcast from society because of the leprosy. His faith made him complete.

The same can happen to us. The Greek sozo literally means saved, healed and delivered. It is the whole package: safe and sound with Jesus, rescued from destruction, restored to health, delivered from oppression, made well, made whole, and complete. The physical healing in the Samaritan caused a chain reaction that brought him inner healing too.

So let us never underestimate the power of a thank you. Giving thanks leads us into a blessed life. On that magnificent day a blessed man rejoiced in thanksgiving, demonstrating to those around him the goodness of God!

Choose life

There is always a choice for us: thankfulness or ingratitude. Ingratitude will pollute our thinking and sour our disposition, yet thankfulness brings a flow from the heart which brings an expectation for God's provision.

Psalm 95 describes the effects of ingratitude over the nation of Israel.

Do not harden your hearts, as at Meribah, as on the day at Massah in the wilderness, when your fathers put me to the test and put me to the proof, though they had seen my work. For forty years I loathed that generation and said, 'They are a people who go astray in their heart, and they have not known my ways.' Therefore I swore in my wrath, 'They shall not enter my rest.' (Psalm 95:8-11 ESV)

It's serious stuff – hardened hearts result in God's wrath and anger. As unbelief insulates us from God's power, ingratitude insulates us from God's blessing. In spite of everything God did for them, the Israelites grumbled against God and his appointed leaders. Though they were out of Egypt, Egypt was clearly not out of them! Time and time again in the wilderness they showed unbelief, complaining, murmuring and outright rebellion.

Paul warned us that what happened to them is an example for us (1 Corinthians 10:6-11). Meribah was a place of quarrelling and Massah a place of testing. Israel's attitude led them a merry chase around the wilderness for forty years. Instead of thanking God for salvation from Egypt, for their daily bread, for quail, for water from rocks, for safety, health and indestructible shoes, they grew hard in heart and they quarrelled. They fell very short of what he wanted for them.

Ingratitude produces cynicism and discouragement. It infects our relationships with each other, and the Lord. Ingratitude clouds our vision and results in spiritual wandering (Numbers 14-16). It can delay or rob us of our destiny; it did in Israel and it will with us.

It is amazing how we do not need to train children to complain, to whine, to moan, to cry needlessly, to be selfish, and so on. They just do all those things naturally! Parents have to teach their children to say please and thank you and to be considerate and kind. We have to train our own hearts to do the same:

Put on then, as God's chosen ones, holy and beloved, compassionate hearts, kindness, humility, meekness, and patience, bearing with one another and, if one has a complaint against another, forgiving each other; as the Lord has forgiven you, so you also must forgive. And above all these put on love, which binds everything together in perfect harmony. And let the peace of Christ rule in your hearts, to which indeed you were called in one body. And be thankful. Let the word of Christ dwell in you richly, teaching and admonishing one another in all wisdom, singing psalms and hymns and spiritual songs, with thankfulness in your hearts to God. And whatever you do, in word or deed, do everything in the name of the Lord Jesus, giving thanks to God the Father through him. (Colossians 3:12-17 ESV)

The attitude of gratitude

Robert Emmons, professor of psychology at the University of California, Davis, has done extensive research on gratitude. He found that people who view life as a gift and consciously acquire an 'attitude of gratitude' will experience multiple advantages. Gratitude improves emotional and physical health, and it can strengthen relationships and communities, so he suggests keeping a gratitude journal, learning prayers of gratitude and using visual reminders.

'Without gratitude, life can be lonely, depressing and impoverished,' Emmons says. 'Gratitude enriches human life. It elevates, energises, inspires and transforms. People are moved, opened and humbled through expressions of gratitude.'

Research also shows that grateful people feel better about their lives, are more optimistic, more energetic, and more enthusiastic. They are more determined, more interested, and more joyful. They exercise more, get more sleep, and have fewer illnesses. They are more likely to help someone else, are clearer thinking and more resilient in tough times, less plagued by stress, live longer, enjoy closer family ties, and more religious.

The barriers to this mind-set are:

- A victim attitude coupled with a sense of entitlement – 'if you believe you're entitled to most things, then you will be thankful for little.'
- Preoccupation with materialism – 'overemphasis on things results in comparisons with those who have more than you do, which leads to resentments that diminish gratefulness.'

- A lack of self-reflection – never taking time to reflect on what you have, just taking things for granted.
- A lack of prior deprivation – if you have been given everything and never known what it is to be without, you can suffer 'affluenza.' When you have much it is harder to be grateful for the little things in life.
- Self-centredness – the self-absorbed have little energy for recognising and appreciating others in ways that express gratitude.

It's a kingdom culture

Gratitude should be the natural attitude for believers and is part of the culture of the kingdom (Colossians 3; Ephesians 5; Romans 12). In worship, gratitude is the attitude that determines our 'altitude.' The condition of our heart determines how 'high' we go; a soft and thankful heart flows easily into the presence of God and soars in the heavenly realm.

Gratitude helps our evangelism. If we are thankful and believe that God is good all the time, it will be a bridge to those who haven't yet discovered Jesus. We affect people around us if we are happy and joyful, and they want to find out what's different about us.

Gratitude also accompanies supernatural multiplication.

Taking the five loaves and the two fish and looking up to heaven, he gave thanks and broke the loaves. Then he gave them to his disciples to distribute to the people. He also divided the two fish among them all. They all ate and were satisfied, and the disciples picked up twelve basketfuls of broken pieces of bread and fish. The number of the men who had eaten was five thousand. (Mark 6:41-44 NIV)

Jesus gave thanks for the provision of just five loaves of bread and two fishes, and then fed a multitude with twelve baskets left over. He didn't moan, 'What use is this paltry amount?' There was no doubt or unbelief in his heart, because he knew his Father was the provider. God delights in abundance, but is never wasteful. I'd like to think that little boy went home with a basket of food for his family that day...

Toys are us!

On a mission trip to a school and children's home in Trincomalee, Sri Lanka, we planned a feast day. We bought food on the way and had collected many small toys and gift items to give away to the children as presents. Donna and I painted murals on the school building while the staff prepared food, and children from the surrounding villages started to arrive for this special celebration.

Before long, the place was jammed with very excited little ones, lined up in orderly rows. Toys were laid out and the children were called forward in groups so they could choose one item. After a while, one of the team members called us in, looking worried – there were three times as many children as we expected and nothing like enough toys for each one.

But as we looked at the children waiting expectantly, we were reminded of Heidi Baker's story of miraculous multiplication of presents in Mozambique. With a very light heart and a huge expectation we thanked God for what he had done before, thanked him for what we had brought with us in our cases and asked him to do a multiplication of gifts again.

Donna and I returned to painting murals outside, but when we came back in later the children excitedly showed us their gifts. Not one of them was without – they were all smiling, laughing and playing around the building. And amazingly there was still plenty left over, so we could give to the teachers and other families too! The children enjoyed a chicken dinner; it was a great and miraculous day.

So thanksgiving has power; it prepares the way for God to show us his salvation and provision. Like David, if we remember what God has done for us and give thanks, it will prepare us to face our next challenge, because God wants to lead us to victory in every situation we face. He also wants us to live in blessing.

The blessing zone

We are called to live in righteousness, peace and joy in the Holy Spirit. Righteousness is a declaration of God's will in on earth and destroys the works of the devil – it's what Jesus came to do. Peace is about being in alignment with God's purposes, and supernatural joy is the conduit of the kingdom coming to earth. You can only give away what you have received, so the way to release joy is to receive joy. And in his presence is fullness of joy (Psalm 16:11)!

In one of his letters, Paul talks of 'three things that remain' – they are 'faith, hope and love' (1 Corinthians 13:13). In this life we have to guard these things very carefully. Francis Frangipane says, 'Every area of our lives that isn't glistening with hope is under the influence of a lie.'

Stop to consider that! How many areas in your life are truly glistening with hope and joyful expectancy? And conversely how many areas are shadowed by clouds of doubt or brushed by a cold wind of fear? The enemy tends to go after our faith, hope and love, so we need to protect them in the garden of our hearts.

Proverbs warns us to guard our hearts as the wellspring of life. We need to weed out the lies and unbelief and tend the precious plants. Faith, hope and love are part of our identity as children of God. They are the seeds of promise that we must nurture through every season of life.

In God we have our being and through him we live and breathe. Christ in us is the hope of glory and the same resurrection power that raised Jesus from the dead is coursing through our veins. His pneuma breathed life into Adam, breathes on us daily, and as he rejoices over us with song, his mercies are new every day.

Remember whose you are and remember who you are. We walk in the truth of his promise over us and his ongoing revelation to us. Thanksgiving leads us into his presence where there is nothing but blessing and favour...

My dear friend and spiritual father Pastor Gary Kantola,

when asked, 'How are you?' whether in church or at the store, would always reply, 'Well, I'm blessed and highly favoured of the Lord.'

That decree came out of his mouth many times every day. 'How are you today, Gary?' 'Well, you know, I'm blessed and highly favoured of the Lord!'

The favour on his life made him a man of vision and influence. He drew pastors and leaders together in a unity that never previously existed in the Lehigh Valley area of Pennsylvania. He was a wonderful man who knew how to laugh and his relationship with Papa God made everyone around him want to know God just the same. I loved to do life with Gary and miss him greatly.

Royal decree

Because we are royalty, we get to make decrees! We are brothers of the King of kings, and royal children of the most High God. As kings and queens in the kingdom we can exercise authority. So if something comes into your life that doesn't look like a blessing, demand it turns into one. If a stumbling block is before you, decree that it becomes a stepping stone to blessing.

There is a delegated authority over our lives for a kingdom purpose. Like Jesus, we should operate under the power and anointing of Holy Spirit.

God anointed Jesus of Nazareth with the Holy Spirit and with power, who went about doing good and healing all who were oppressed by the devil, for God was with him. (Acts 10:38 NKJV)

Generosity

Sowing and reaping, and generously giving are part of kingdom culture. When we do these things with intent and purpose it also releases blessing. The measure we give out will be the measure we receive back. Withholding from the Lord produces nothing. A poverty spirit is an ungodly spirit, but giving brings release in ways we may not even be aware of.

The tithe is the first-fruits of our income and the kingdom principle of giving is that the first-fruits go into the storehouse so there is food in the house. The storehouse is the local church – the family we belong to, where we grow together. God also sends us from there to do the stuff of the kingdom, distributing the bounty of heaven.

The Bible says the tithe is holy, so don't redirect it somewhere else. It is designated for kingdom purpose and as believers we are blessed when we obey the commands of the Lord. When we honour God with our giving, we will see the true riches of heaven.

Giving is a physical act that brings a spiritual release. Everything belongs to God, but he wants to see what we do with it to develop our character. Radical generosity is the next step. When we learn how to give his way, heaven is unsuppressed and we will live in the blessing zone.

So as we enter his gates with thanksgiving and come into his courts with praise, we are called into our destiny. Worship brings an invitation from heaven to come closer, where God's plans and purposes for our lives are revealed, and there is opportunity for recalibration, healing and restoration.

What Jesus accomplished for us deserves our praise for all eternity. Joy overflows because the reward has already been received, a ransom price paid in full! A kingly decree said that only priests could carry the presence forever (1 Chronicles 15:2). So the promise is that we, God's royal priesthood, are on this earth to be carriers of his presence wherever we go.

The presence brings blessing

When we shout for joy in exuberance, we bring fruitfulness into dark and barren places. As the Ark of the Covenant lay waiting at the house of Obed-Edom (2 Samuel 6:11), his whole household prospered. How much more blessing is there, when we intentionally go about spreading the love of the Lord? We carry his glory so that we can bring transformation to others! As God's yielded people we get to define and change the culture around us by the way we live our lives. We can carry the victory of his presence into every situation. A thankful heart will draw what is destined for our future into our present.

Activate gratitude

Give yourself a thirty-minute thanksgiving break with God. The rules are simple – no requests, no petitions, no asking for anything and certainly no complaining! Just give him thanks and see where it leads you. Mark the time when you start and see if you even notice when thirty minutes has passed!

Some more ways to activate gratitude in your life:

1. Thanksgiving walk – take a stroll to remember what God has done in your life and give thanks while you are doing it.

2. Thirty-second break – If you are really busy, turn your affection to God for just half a minute and thank him for who he is. If something good happens during the day, stop for a moment and appreciate God for what he has done. Notice and give thanks for the little things.

3. End of day reflections – take a little time in the evening to say thank you; some do it with their children around the meal table. Find at least three things from the day you can be thankful for.

4. Sing your gratitude – while you walk, in the shower, driving the car.

5. Write a card – find someone you want to thank, take the time to write out your thanks and a personal message. If possible deliver it in person and tell them why you think they are so special.

6. Journal – keep a record of thanksgiving and gratitude to value what God has done in your life, and then look back and remember. If you write down three things a day that you're thankful for, at the end of the year that's over a thousand thanks!

7. Tell someone – speak your gratitude in person and tell somebody what you are thankful to God for; it encourages more testimony!

8. Be grateful – be the type of person who lives thankfully in your worship, in your relationships, in your whole life's message.

12

MORE THAN A SONG

CREATIVE EXPRESSIONS OF WORSHIP

Any given Sunday

Traditional church bells peal, calling a sleepy English country parish to worship...People step off a busy high street into a church, to be welcomed by the friendly greeters at the door...A large car park is filling up as families and young people spill out, eager to greet friends and find their way into the sanctuary...A school hall is slowly transformed into a church as the hubbub of conversations builds over coffee and the band tunes up...

The vicar stands and says 'turn to hymn number 95 in your songbooks,' the minister announces, 'the words of the songs will be on the screen behind me'... the worship leader strikes up the first chord and invites the congregation, 'Let's have a time of worship,' and all over the country corporate worship has begun. For the majority of those church services, the 'time of worship' will entail singing songs.

Now I love singing and writing songs. It's exciting when one of my songs is played on the radio or by another worship team, or someone hits one of my tunes on YouTube. Songs are such a wonderful expression of love, feeling, truth, liturgy, belief and prophetic decree. Yet there are still so many more ways to worship our God. The Creator created us to be creative!

This wondrous blue-green ball of ours is absolutely jammed with life. Scientists estimate there are approximately 400,000 flowering plant species, over 23,000 types of tree, 925,000 species of insect, 28,000 species of fish, 50,000 types of vertebrates and for some reason God wanted a lot of beetles – over 340,000 separate types of beetle have been identified – and so I could go on. He is extravagantly expressive and amazingly abundant.

We who are designed in his image should abound creatively too! So let's stop limiting ourselves in how we express our hearts and gratitude to the King of the universe. We can bring 'more than a song,' as Matt Redman puts it.

God loves our uniqueness. Every snowflake, leaf and flower petal, has its own personal design reflecting the diversity of the Creator. An Ordnance Survey map shows the curving contour lines of the earth, like a giant fingerprint, with no two bumps the same. Neither are we. All creation waits in anticipation for us to realise who we are and to rise and shine (Romans 8:19; Isaiah 60:1)!

I love looking at the majestic flourish of God's paintbrush in the sky and find that every sunset is different. So why do many worship bands end up sounding the same? Perhaps plagiarism is the finest form of flattery, which would also explain why cover bands are so popular!

I'm not just an echo, I have a voice. Sometimes it's been shut down, rejected, refused, even totally lost. But even when my calling and purpose on the earth is being resisted, I will stand firm in who God says I am. I will lift up my voice to him.

Onward Christian soldiers

A critical attitude is death to the creative heart. Positive critiquing in a loving relationship is biblical and part of discipleship and mentoring, but negative criticism is fuel for the demonic and it kills. It has no place in a thriving kingdom culture and certainly not in any worship team.

Of course leaders of worship need to sift through songs for their congregation based on content, theology, melody, lyrics and style; not all songs seem the right fit for a given context. But getting on a soap box and attacking the latest album, arrangement, vocal style, or worshipper is simply inappropriate.

It's not good to see people excluded from a particular 'club' (network of churches), or to hear worship teams puffing themselves up over how much better they are than the next one along the road in a competitive spirit. We need to give each other the same grace we would like for ourselves, and realise that Jesus prayed for our unity in all things (John 17:20-26).

My experience is that worship teams combined from many different church families can command an extraordinary blessing, helping us grasp the greater reality of God's plan. The Father's desire is for not just a few, but for all his children to come home. And when we gather in his house we should play nicely together! We have different styles, but are all on the same team.

(Father I pray that) that they may all be one; even as you, Father, are in me and I in you, that they also may be in us, so that the world may believe that you sent me. The glory which you have given me I have given to them, that they may be one, just as we are one. (John 17:21-22 NASB)

This profound prayer was among the last words of Jesus to his disciples before he was crucified. How much attention, though, do we pay to them? We are not supposed to be uniform, so feel free to express yourselves But we need to show the world we're one, as Jesus and the Father are one, not solitary 'Lone Rangers.'

Let's stop the friendly fire, competition and criticism, and replace them with honour and celebration. Recognising the glory in one another releases the life of heaven. It's time to stand shoulder to shoulder, our shields locked together like a Roman infantry 'wedge,' with our swords pointing towards the enemy, instead of stabbing at our own.

There is one hope, one faith, one truth, and one Lord over all (Ephesians 4:4). We need to put our energy into agreement instead of argument. I long to see the body of Christ devoting herself to the promise of heaven instead of protesting and quarrelling.

There is such power in agreement and the blessing of Psalm 133 is for us all. When we repent about the way we think about these things, we will see transformation, because there is so much more than we have already tasted and seen. We were never meant to be so content with so little!

Wake up and get dressed!
Awake, awake, put on your strength, put on your beautiful garments, shake yourself from the dust, loose the bonds from your neck and arise! (from Isaiah 52:1-2)

As we put on our kingdom clothing, we display the glory of Jesus and people will definitely like what they see.

These days in more contemporary worship settings, images are superimposed behind words and video clips are regular part of worship. Some churches have camera crews and lighting rigs like theatre venues or TV studios! Others give space for painting during the worship time and make room so dancers have space to move. We should remember that all artists are seers, with prophetic qualities. They can speak God's 'now' word into situations.

Of course, not everyone who picks up a brush as an act of worship will have their work critically acclaimed and ending up in a gallery, just as not everyone who pens a song will receive a Grammy. But if we confine expressions of worship to a few styles and a few select individuals, we miss an array of expression that reflects the heart and nature of the creator.

There are testimonies of people who have looked at prophetic paintings and been so deeply touched that a part of their heart was mended or a physical pain left. Our love offerings to the Lord can release the miraculous in his presence.

In his presence is the power to heal

Is it surprising that the Creator can use the brushstrokes of a faithful hand to bring healing or deliverance? We know that Peter's shadow and pieces of Paul's clothing sent to the sick released healing. Prayer cloths these days are commonplace and I've even heard of a scanned prayer cloth faxed to a sick child in another country that released a mighty miracle!

I've personally blessed a friend ministering in India while I was in the United States by taking a picture of my hand and sending it to him as a picture message, as I couldn't lay hands on him before he left. It had the desired effect: a Holy Spirit touch, bringing courage and clarity before he stepped up to minister to the congregation there.

These days we can reach out to people over the internet, using Skype and other modern means of communication. For me it is part of the 'even greater' way we fulfil Jesus' commission with our imagination, grace gifts and anointing.

Let's dance

I normally leave dancing to those with better coordination than me! But movement is such a good way of expressing something more. We are not expecting a flash mob in a worship service (although that would be amazing), but freedom of movement and expression are key. Dance can speak prophetically.

In the healing rooms at Bethel church in Redding, California, I was transfixed by the dance leader followed by dancing children. They emulated her by jumping, twisting and swirling around those waiting to be prayed for, like a school of dolphins playing around a boat. As they swept past, I could feel a lightness come over me. It was as if they were washing away doubts and fears in the room with their flowing and sometimes playful movements.

It was beautiful to behold that a special part of the creative worship. There is no 'junior' Holy Spirit; his anointing on his little children released something very powerful indeed.

There are some YouTube videos out there satirising the feeble attempts of Christians to move their bodies in worship. We end up poking fun at something because we haven't fully understood its significance. When fear of man kills our creative expression, we will struggle to break into the kind of worship that brings glory to God, shakes the heavenly realm and transforms people and places.

Ways of worship

David found many varied ways to worship the Lord, and the psalms are full of expressive praise movements and physical responses. This short list of words are simply translated 'praise' in English, but have such a greater depth of meaning in Hebrew.

Barak – to kneel or bow, to give reverence to God as an act of adoration

Guwl – to spin around, under the influence of any violent emotion

Shachah – to prostrate in homage or loyalty to God, bow down, fall down flat

Shuwr – strolling minstrels

Todah – an extension of the hand, adoration

Yadah – to hold out the hand, to revere or worship with extended hands

Alats/Alaz – to jump for joy, exult, be joyful, rejoice, and triumph

Anah – to heed, pay attention, to respond, to begin to speak, to testify

Chagag – to move in a circle, to march in a sacred procession, to be giddy

Chuwl – to twist or whirl in a circular spiral manner

Dagal – to raise a flag, to be conspicuous, set up with banners

Kara – to bend the knee, to sink, to prostrate, bow down, bring down low

Karar – to whirl

Macha – to rub or strike the hands together in exultation, clap

Machowl – a round dance

Ragad – to stamp, to spring about wildly or for joy, to shout aloud and make a noise

Taga – to clatter, slap hands together, clang an instrument, blow a trumpet

These are all physical responses in praise. Clapping, singing, raising hands, awkwardly stepping from one foot to the other are all common in the kind of meetings I go to. We also see dancing, painting, flag-waving and so on, but there are many more ways of worshipping our great God.

The first time I went to Columbia I was blown away by the passion and exuberance of the worship. This joyful gathering was more like a party or concert than a church service, but with people of all ages. In one particular church in Medellin they shouted and danced, sang and jumped around because they knew what price had been paid. He who has been forgiven much loves much! Many had been saved from tough circumstances – from drug and alcohol abuse, prostitution and poverty.

This church might not be to everyone's taste, but it was full of life and laughter. And in the attractive environment of his presence, hundreds more people were healed, saved and delivered. The world wants that kind of experience.

Of course Columbia has a different culture to reserved old England, but we are still worshipping the same King! The Father loves it when his children enjoy themselves, when they feel free to express themselves. We can enjoy the music and dancing to celebrate who God is.

That same year at the Global Awakening Youth Power Invasion event in Brazil I once again witnessed passionate praise from young (and not so young!) people. It was so compelling, I wanted to capture something of that freedom and passion and bring it back home.

In a conference we were leading in Vietnam, when we said 'Let us pray,' we could barely hear ourselves think over the voices of those assembled! They raised the roof with petitions and pleas to the throne room just as they spent themselves during the times of worship. Different nations and cultures have so much to offer each other.

We must create an environment where people may express themselves without being judged. If all we do is sit in judgement, then we will bring an offence instead of an offering! It's never good to boo from the side lines instead of getting stuck in. We can shape the culture by our heart response, our encouragement and our attitudes.

In his speech 'Citizens in a Republic,' Theodore Roosevelt delivered these powerful words. As a young man he caught my warrior heart and I've kept a little card with these words in my Bible:

It is not the critic who counts; not the man who points out how the strong man stumbles, or where the doer of deeds could have done them better. The credit belongs to the man who is actually in the arena, whose face is marred by dust and sweat and blood; who strives valiantly; who errs, who comes short again and again, because there is no effort without error and shortcoming; but who does actually strive to do the deeds; who knows great enthusiasms, the great devotions; who spends himself in a worthy cause; who at the best knows in the end the triumph of high achievement, and who at the worst, if he fails, at least fails while daring greatly, so that his place shall never be with those cold and timid souls who neither know victory nor defeat.

We are on this planet to spend ourselves in high devotion and what cause is more worthy than the authentic gospel of Jesus Christ? To bring good news to the poor, to dare greatly when given the opportunity, to risk everything for the possibility of seeing a life touched, healed and delivered!

Prescribed offerings

The Lord gave Moses many varied and detailed commandments about the way Israel's offerings were to be made in the wilderness years: burnt offerings, grain offerings, sin offerings, guilt offerings, ordination offerings and the peace offering (see Leviticus 1-7).

The attention to detail is very interesting as it specifies how each offering is to be placed on the altar, the way the animal is to be divided and which parts are to be used, the manner in which it would be consumed and even the type of clothing to be worn in the tidying up afterwards! It mattered to God that his people could offer appropriate and acceptable sacrifices.

The animals offered were to be without blemish or defect. Only the finest flour was used, and just the first fruits of the grain, so the offering would be not mediocre but excellent – as Jesus was the sinless one making a perfect offering on our behalf. Key ingredients like salt or frankincense were added before the sacrifice was placed on the altar to be burned, raising a sweet aroma to the Lord. Our offerings also must be well-prepared and fragrant.

When Jesus was at the temple in Jerusalem he observed an old widow making an offering:

And he (Jesus) sat down opposite the treasury and watched the people putting money into the offering box. Many rich people put in large sums. And a poor widow came and put in two small copper coins, which make a penny. And he called his disciples to him and said to them, 'Truly, I say to you, this poor widow has put in more than all those who are contributing to the offering box. For they all contributed out of their abundance, but she out of her poverty has put in everything she had, all she had to live on.' (Mark 12:41-44 ESV)

Jesus observed the widow giving sacrificially, knew they were her last coppers, and recognised the true value of her gift. He saw to the heart of issues.

And the scribe said to him, 'You are right, Teacher. You have truly said that he is one, and there is no other besides him. And to love him with all the heart and with all the understanding and with all the strength, and to love one's neighbour as oneself, is much more than all whole burnt offerings and sacrifices.' And when Jesus saw that he answered wisely, he said to him, 'You are not far from the kingdom of God.' And after that no one dared to ask him any more questions. (Mark 12:32-34 ESV)

The greatest commandments, to love the Lord and those around you, was recognised by one Scribe as more important than those carefully prescribed burnt offerings and sacrifices laid out in the law. Jesus silenced the questions by confirming this man's personal revelation: 'You are not far from the kingdom of God.'

Jesus' teaching echoed Amos' cry about God not receiving their offerings because of their neglect of the poor. Our kindness, love, and sacrificial support of others are a sweet fragrance to the Lord and demonstrations of the kingdom of heaven on earth.

Worship offerings

For many years I have wanted to create a church environment where all types of offering can be brought before the Lord and the family. According to Leviticus, some people may only be able to afford to bring a modest grain offering or a pigeon, others a goat and others a more extravagant bull, yet all these offerings are acceptable to God and should be acceptable to us.

Over the last twenty years we have held special gatherings for a varied worship offering time. We don't do this every week, but it is a regular part of our calendar. We have no band or speaker, just a family gathering where each one is given the space to bring their personal offering to God. The idea is to release creativity in many forms and to encourage individuals to have a voice in the family, to express something of their heart before others.

Some of these 'Worship Offering' evenings have been simple, left open to the flow of the Holy Spirit, and others have been based on a theme and a journey. They have all been incredibly creative, poignant and humbling. I love the fact that there is no agenda, other than to bring a personal offering. It is an empowering, grace-filled time, helping even the quietest person to bring their 'grain offering' as a sweet aroma to the Lord.

In the atmosphere of gratitude and praise we encourage everybody to leave the fear of man at the door, because we want our gathering place to be holy ground. There is no competition, no grading, no weighing of one against another, just creative expressions of the heart.

Some sing, some dance, some bring a spoken word, some place pictures around the room or photographs they've taken, some bring a painting and describe what it means. Some have baked, knitted and sewn, others bring a creative communion for all to share, some share a simple thought or reflection. We simply make space for a flow from earth to heaven and heaven to earth. We want people to bring an offering of thanks to God, not a mini-preach to the church!

One of our themes was Father's Day, when we asked our people to prepare by considering what would we want to say to our heavenly Dad, and how would we like to say it? The gifts that were brought to the 'altar' were many and varied, from an exuberant adult bringing his childlike drawing saying 'Daddy, look what I painted for you,' to carefully crafted poems, paintings and testimonies that uncover usually hidden hearts.

Poems and pictures reveal the heart of children adopted into an incredible family. It has been precious seeing a young man who had previously only ever sung in his bedroom sing to the church, and hearing a spoken word from one who had once been very broken, a grateful story from someone who had suffered pain and a bold decree from one previously so timid, all testimonies of transformation.

The overflow of worship brings a community closer together,

with a clearer understanding of each individual's journey. These stories become part of our corporate memory. Though usually reserved for one-to-one encounters, shared publicly they draw the church into a deeper sense of unity and purpose.

Excellence versus perfectionism

We are here to show a more excellent way – not perfectionism but excellence. We want to break out of mediocrity, without slipping into striving. I did a little workshop recently with my Worship Expressions team on this theme in the context of the kingdom and life attitudes. Here are some of the responses:

Perfectionism is striving without grace, trying to achieve from a warped need for approval.. It is struggling in your own strength to achieve a preconceived standard that no one notices but you... It is focusing on what you haven't become or achieved yet and where you've failed... It is selfish and inward focused...It comes from pride and is about exalting yourself...It is a one-man rat race, and smells of rotten eggs!

Perfection is never reached so it makes you feel inadequate and a failure...It is a driven behaviour, exhausting and not really achievable...It's based on a belief that it all depends on our own efforts...It is trying to please others, driven by a fear of not being good enough... It's like hitting a brick wall and never scaling it...It is seeing perfection as something to be attained in the future rather than the past tense: *'By one sacrifice he has made perfect forever those who are being made holy'* (Hebrews 10:14, NIV).

Perfectionism is a pursuit of a false surface reality: like trying to win a trophy that turns out to be cheap gaudy plastic. It's an endless list of contradicting opposites, a sliding scale where equilibrium can never quite be reached because there are too many unquantifiable variables. The perfect state is subjective; everyone's eyes are trained to recognise different patterns and therefore see different faults. Even if someone deemed you perfect, somebody else would say you had a lot more learning to do!

Perfectionism is trying to reach something that's forever out of your grasp...It is a driven behaviour borne out of a need for approval...It is neurotic and stressful... It's unattainable because like the wind, you cannot catch it...

Excellence is to show forth God's glory on your life...It is to rest, knowing who you are in him, already made perfect in Jesus...It is knowing your identity in the family and that you are approved... It gives a sense of satisfaction.

Excellence is listening to and obeying his words. It is giving yourself totally to God, allowing him to mould you to be who you were made to be, and achieve the things he wants you to achieve; his work, not ours. It's OK if it takes time. Excellence allows you to achieve your potential with teamwork and with the help of Daddy God...

Excellence is focusing on the ultimate in positivity: God... Excellence is a way (1 Corinthians 12:31) and the way of excellence is love (1 Corinthians 13)...Philippians 4:8 is excellence: doing something to the best of your ability without striving. Excellence is being more than a conqueror.

Excellence comes from a commitment to be as outstanding and brilliant as my gifts, skills and calling will allow...It happens when I 'let go' of my old corrupted self, and run with the Holy Spirit filling my new self (as in 1 Corinthians 9:24 and Hebrews 12:1) like a spiritual Olympian, or perhaps I should say a Para-Olympian now – I dared to wrestled with God and now I've got a limp!

Excellence is born out of your energy and skill and creativity, working in harmony...It's going the extra mile, but also knowing when to stop...It comes from pouring your whole heart in, getting help to hone your skill, spending time on your practice, being okay with mistakes...It is applying yourself, challenging yourself, refining and pruning.

Excellence comes from a heart adjusted to honour and love. An excellent heart pours out goodness. Our purpose is to get close to God's heart, to choose to be known by him and to go through a process he likes – the journey of the heart. Excellence smells like sweet honey...Mmm, more, please!

Keep the home fires burning

In the order for offerings laid out in Leviticus, there is a clear command: the fire is to be kept burning at all times (Leviticus 6:12)! God originally lit the fire on the altar (9:24) but it is the role of the priest to make sure it does not go out, even when the ashes have to be carried away. Modern-day Levites are called to burn with a passionate fire that doesn't get snuffed out. 1 John 5:21 captures it so simply:

Little children, keep yourself from things that might take God's place in your heart.

It is usually translated as 'keep yourselves from idols,' but the words above from the New Living Translation speak volumes to me. Idolatry is constructing false gods to legitimise what we do. We are all children of a good Dad, so why not let life flow out of that? Avoid at all costs anything that occupies your heart, that replaces your affection for God!

Jesus' last words to his disciples clearly instructed them to wait for the power they would receive in the baptism of the Holy Spirit (Acts 1). They needed the energising Spirit to fulfil the assignment Jesus had given them, so they could live and serve in the promised presence of God.

Wait on God

To wait is to worship, to linger in his presence, to hang out near his glory...

The man who took Israel into the Promised Land didn't depart from the temple or leave the presence of God (Exodus 33:10-11). Joshua was transformed by the pillar of fire and the glory cloud. So from his time of spying out Canaan (Numbers 13) right through to leading a nation across the Jordan (Joshua 1), he valued the presence of God. He learnt how to hear the voice and was prepared ultimately to take the place of Moses leading the people of Israel.

Something happens to us in his manifest presence. I feel it every time and there's no place I'd rather be! The devil is trying to take Holy Spirit out of the church so that it will take heaven out of earth, but we are instructed to resist him and choose a Spirit-filled life.

When Jesus spoke, his words released life, and he is still speaking today. 'Be still and know that I am God...' In other words, sit down, wait, and listen! 'Be still' is a summons to encounter the Lord himself. It is intimate but we need to know God as he wants to know us.

Stop the busyness ... come aside and wait. God speaks to birth his promises and purposes in our lives – just as Adam 'knew' Eve and she brought forth a son. We need to rediscover the power of Biblical meditation. Several groups in Southampton meet under the banner of 'Gold in the City' for contemplative prayer and a time of silence amidst the noise of life. They step aside to pray, meditate and listen the voice that burned in the bush.

Others like to 'soak' in the glory by finding a still place, listening to gentle music, and tuning into the Spirit of the living God. When we wait on God we get to fill our minds with truth as we turn all our attention on him and let our affections flow out. If we don't take time we will not fully capture the potential he has for us.

We are seated in heavenly places with God. As we sit with the Father, we can reflect on his truth and his word. We make a space for Holy Spirit to bring fresh revelation and drop into our spirit something we would not get any other way. His reality should be so much more attractive than any of the world's distractions.

So let each one of us wait and listen, and allow God's words of life to shape our lives. Then we can pour out from hearts overwhelmed by his wisdom, goodness and love.

13
LET YOUR GLORY FALL
DAVID'S LEGACY

Over the years I've sampled many different styles and forms of music and played thousands of different songs. But what draws me nearest to God is the spontaneous song of the heart.

The sound of heaven

There have been times in large gatherings when the overflow seems unending and we just sing and sing to the Lord. Once in Brazil we worshiped until, one by one, the band left the stage and joined the congregation in singing. This spontaneous worship went on for almost an hour; I wasn't clock watching but was caught up in the sound of heaven.

Another time in Lakeland, Florida a corporate shout began that seemed like it would never stop. We were coming to the end of a set while worshipping when a great cry came up from the congregation. This shout of joyful, exuberant praise rose and fell, rose and fell, like ocean waves of praise crashing on the altar of grace.

The meeting host came to the front of the stage but seemed to be lost in wonder and lost for words, so he just let what was going on in the room continue. It was powerful and heart-transforming, and a prelude to a powerful outpouring of Holy Spirit. There seemed to be angels swooping back and forth above us as we roared our adoration to the King of kings!

I personally felt touched by the Lord in this atmosphere, as if something had fallen on me and pressed me between the seats for almost two hours, with the power of God pulsing through my body like electricity. I had visions and heard God speak to my heart deeply in this encounter.

When we returned from Lakeland we had some of the most powerful healing services I have ever experienced in my city. It was a sovereign move of the Holy Spirit, the like of which I have never witnessed there before. The worship was intense and incredibly joyful, the ministry was wonderful and we witnessed the kindness of God time and time again.

Every Monday night for months, so many hungry people came and I personally laid hands on several hundred every week. People were powerfully touched by Holy Spirit, there were significant words of prophecy and encouragement and we witnessed many significant healings, even medically verified miracles. One lady in her late fifties received a brand-new heart! After tests to verify results (the equipment was thought to be faulty), the heart consultant told her that her heart was in better condition than his was!

My wife and I prayed with another young lady whose ovary had been removed because of a grapefruit-sized cyst. A few days after we laid hands on her she had an ultrasound scan and the technician told her that both of her ovaries were perfect! She had received a creative miracle and we give Jesus all the glory and honour.

The glory falls

There have also been many occasions when his glory drops on us like a deluge and we can barely stand. At other times, the sense of God's presence has been so amazing that one by one, we in the band stop playing until we have holy silence. These are profound, holy moments when God came so near we didn't want to do anything to touch his glory...

And it came to pass when the priests came out of the Most Holy Place (for all the priests who were present had sanctified themselves, without keeping to their divisions), and the Levites who were the singers, all those of Asaph and Heman and Jeduthun, with their sons and their brethren, stood at the east end of the altar, clothed in white linen, having cymbals, stringed instruments and harps, and with them one hundred and twenty priests sounding with trumpets indeed it came to pass, when the trumpeters and singers were as one, to make one sound to be heard in praising and thanking the Lord, and when they lifted up their voice with the trumpets and cymbals and instruments of music, and praised the Lord, saying: 'For he is good, for his mercy endures forever,' that the house, the house of the Lord, was filled with a cloud, so that the priests could not continue ministering because of the cloud; for the glory of the Lord filled the house of God. (2 Chronicles 5:11-14 NKJV)

When the glory of the Lord filled the house of God the priests could no longer minister – there's a benchmark for corporate worship gatherings! The presence of our holy God can manifest so powerfully that we can no longer stand but only fall face-down. Moments like that are extremely precious and I treasure each time.

The father's son

When King Solomon dedicated the temple to the Lord, it was the culmination of his father's legacy. Solomon built on David's plans, vision and direction using the resources he had provided. The son stepped into the dream of the father, the culmination of David's lifetime of adoring his God. So the passion of the man after God's own heart exploded into the next generation.

A good person leaves an inheritance for their children's children. (Proverbs 13:22, NIV)

Despite these familiar words, so often in church history people have sought to disconnect from their forefathers. The Protestant church has indeed been built on protest! As people disagreed on doctrine a new church was formed. Some, like Wesley, were forced out of the established church because the call of God on their lives was not welcome. But kingdom values include honouring our heritage.

These days we are witnessing a fresh emphasis on connectedness and relationship, so people are gathering around spiritual mothers and fathers. This means that when there are disagreements over doctrinal issues, it doesn't have to cause division. The poles of relationship support our ark of agreement and covenant.

Building on good foundations

Paul described himself as a master builder (1 Corinthians 3:10-17) and encouraged us to build wisely on his foundations. When we honour it releases life, so that life and blessings flow as we keep building on the good.

God wants us to learn how to live the Christian life multi-generationally. Instead of tearing up the blueprints and starting from scratch, we can build the kingdom of heaven as family: grandparents, parents, children, grandchildren, and great grandchildren. Job's final years were spent with four generations on the earth (Job 42), a prophetic picture of a beautiful church family.

Legacy and inheritance

We need to celebrate our inheritance, not dismiss it arrogantly. Inheritance can take us out of poverty and into fruitfulness in just a generation. In the UK we have a rich spiritual inheritance and should celebrate the success of spiritual fathers, instead of cynically criticising their weaknesses. When we do that, God can quickly advance us.

By leaving kingdom principles strewn in the rubble, we miss out on the bounty that God has for us. The orphan-hearted nature can cause striving, jealousy, insecurity and an inability to collaborate. Our environment should encourage sons and daughters to express themselves unfettered.

When you find out who you truly are, then everything you do becomes ministry to God. Bill Johnson says, 'The presence of God is the womb out of which dreams are birthed.' The presence is full of promise, and in that atmosphere, the impossible gets released into the earth.

It's a love thing

What I have seen in vision, dreamt with God about, studied, pursued, trained others in and experienced in other parts of the world is to honour the presence of God in worship and pursue his kingdom wholeheartedly. Simply put, it is to be the beloved.

Before anything else, our responsibility is to love and be loved in return. God is love, and he loves love, and loves us. That love is too high, too deep and too long to measure (Ephesians 3:17-19), yet we get to experience it daily. When we are loved like that it changes how we think, how we feel and how we behave.

Our primary role on earth is to live in God's love and then give it away. We are not orphans hoping for a hand-out, but sons and daughters feasting around a table laid for us by the Father. There is no place in our hearts anymore for fear, only space for his perfect love. We step into Christ and become the beloved.

My heart is that we would be kingdom-focused instead of empire building. A 'spirit of empire' strangles moves of God when insecure leadership structures control rather than release. That leaves people spiritually bereft, abused and running from the very thing they need to be part of, church family. The Romans imposed their will with sword and spear all across Europe. And yes, there were benefits, but earthly empire-building is the antithesis of God's kingdom culture.

The power of unity

All around the world humble hearts are going after the kingdom of heaven and the authentic ministry of Jesus is being restored. There is no posturing for position because the leadership are serving, not being served. When people come together in unity, something extremely special happens, just as it did when the musicians and singers played as one in Solomon's temple!

How good and pleasant it is when God's people live together in unity! It is like precious oil poured on the head, running down on the beard, running down on Aaron's beard, down on the collar of his robe. It is as if the dew of Hermon were falling on Mount Zion, for there the Lord bestows his blessing, even life for evermore. (Psalm 133 NIV)

Unity is doing life together well. It brings an anointing from heaven likened to the beautiful anointing oil of the tabernacle. That anointing can break the heavy yoke of heaviness and oppression and bring about blessing and a joy-filled life.

When the disciples gathered to wait in the upper room, they were of one accord. It was then that the Spirit of the Lord fell in an unprecedented way:

When the day of Pentecost had fully come, they were all with one accord in one place. And suddenly there came a sound from heaven, as of a rushing mighty wind, and it filled the whole house where they were sitting. Then there appeared to them divided tongues, as of fire, and one sat upon each of them. And they were all filled with the Holy Spirit and began to speak with other tongues, as the Spirit gave them utterance. (Acts 2:1-4 NKJV)

They had heard the word of the Lord to wait, and they had obeyed and waited. The rest, as they say, is his story!

The dedication of the temple

When Solomon called the nation of Israel together to dedicate the temple it was the culmination of all his father had spent his life preparing for: collecting the materials, saving gold and silver in the treasury and preparing the designs for every aspect of construction. He didn't rebel and say: 'I'm not building that, it's too showy,' or 'I'll keep the gold in the treasury for a rainy day.' A poverty mind-set was not an issue for David or Solomon!

David had seen the Lord of breakthrough bring him victory against his enemies, win peace for Israel and gain them unheard-of prosperity. He made provision for the future and Solomon ran with it. David's mantle was to claim for Israel what was promised to Moses. He told Solomon to ask for wisdom and this was his testimony:

But now the Lord my God has given me rest on every side; there is neither adversary nor evil occurrence. (1 Kings 5:4 NKJV)

Solomon had peace on every border and nothing bad went on, so his police force must have been redundant and spent their time on the golf course!

In my city, when the Street Pastors go about their assignment to bring love to the party-goers and clubbers, there are fewer disturbances, less fighting, fewer 999 calls and fewer people in Accident and Emergency! The council and the police know the statistics and have even put aside finances to help the ongoing funding, which is a remarkable thing in this time of tight budgets.

When we go about doing good, there are fewer evil occurrences. Years ago during 'March for Jesus' with Graham Kendrick, police forces across the nation reported that their phones stopped ringing while the marches were on and for some time afterwards. Something happens when God's people make themselves known in their towns, and it is happening again with initiatives like Healing on the Streets and Burn 24/7. As praise and prayer spill onto the highways and byways, the atmosphere changes.

Solomon's wisdom and management of his father's kingdom was internationally known and brought about incredible prosperity. His proverbs were used by parents to instruct their children as they entered the adult life of responsibilities. Wisdom is a gift passed from generation to generation. It is an inheritance not to be wasted or squandered, but to be built on and added to.

But, let us finally return to the dedication of the temple of Solomon... The nation of Israel gathered in Jerusalem for a celebration that lasted many days. As the Ark of the Covenant came before them, hundreds of priests sacrificed more sheep and oxen than could be counted.

The Ark was placed into the inner sanctuary of the temple. The musicians and singers sang and played, 'God is good and his love and mercy endures forever' (Psalm 136). And their unity brought the cloud of 'Shekinah glory' (1 Kings 8, 2 Chronicles 5). The Shekinah glory is the manifestation of the majestic presence of God in which he descends to dwell among men, when the invisible God becomes visible, and the omnipresence of God is localised.

A nation watched in wonderment as the shining cloud of God descended, just as he had done hundreds of years before on Mount Sinai. In that holy moment the priests ceased their sacrifices, the musicians set down their instruments and the singers stopped their singing. Everyone fell to their faces in awe and worshipped their magnificent God. It was one of the most significant things to happen in Israel's history.

Solomon eventually spoke to the assembly of Israel (possibly two million people). Describing what was happening, and reminding the nation of their history with their God, he spoke about his father David's reign and warned them to remain faithful and follow God's ways.

When Solomon had finished praying, fire came down from heaven and consumed the burnt offering and the sacrifices; and the glory of the Lord filled the temple. And the priests could not enter the house of the Lord, because the glory of the Lord had filled the Lord's house. When all the children of Israel saw how the fire came down, and the glory of the Lord on the temple, they bowed their faces to the ground on the pavement, and worshiped and praised the Lord, saying: *'For he is good, for his mercy endures forever.'* (2 Chronicles 7:1-3, NKJV)

God consumed their offering with fire. All offerings acceptable to the Lord get consumed by his fire and in these days his holy fire is falling on the earth, and on us earthen vessels.

Acceptable extravagance

The celebration was beyond extravagant. If the number of 'uncountable' sacrifices is twice those that were counted, 420,000 animals were offered up to God at that dedication. If every sacrificial ritual required ten minutes to perform, this process would require 7,000 hours. To fit into seven days, it would take 800 priests performing sacrificial duties on 12-hour shifts, serving 24 hours a day – and all at a cost of around £100 million!

Extravagant it was, but God blessed Solomon's reign with the greatest wealth and prosperity ever known in Israel (1 Kings 10, 2 Chronicles 9). He became the wealthiest person on the earth, so much so that silver had little or no value in Jerusalem!

With the measure we pour out, God measures back to us the same. So are we extravagant in our praise...or are we holding back? We might want to give more of our time, our talent, and our treasure, considering how hard it is to out-give a good and generous God.

The dedication of the temple was loud, long, emotional and repetitious, and recent revivals show a similar scenario. There are shiny, happy people having fun, great joy, loud celebrations, emotional singing with repetition and spontaneity (even repeating a chorus more than once!). The fruit is abundant, so the blessing spreads.

There has been much criticism about that kind of worship in recent years. But rather than celebrating critics, I would prefer to celebrate Jesus. Whatever we think, scripture tells us that God showed his approval of the extravagance in Solomon's temple with a divine visitation of his glorious presence.

All ages gathered to worship God as the whole nation came together for this momentous event, and it pleased the Lord. We too are his royal priesthood, his holy nation, called to bring our spiritual offerings that are just waiting to be consumed by holy fire.

Under the old covenant a stone building, animal blood and the singing of David's prayers ushered in the presence of God so powerfully that the glory fire of God filled the temple. So what might happen when human temples, washed by the blood of the Son of God, gather in unity and worship wholeheartedly? What might happen when we thunder the glories of our King extravagantly with one voice?

May you be inspired and encouraged, uplifted and propelled into all the good things God has for you to do. Be a carrier of his promise, and a lover of his presence.
Alun Leppitt.